From
Jea

Praise for
WATCHMAN PRAYER

How different America would be today if only we, as believers in Christ, had been on the lookout for attacks on our country's spiritual well-being! In *Watchman Prayer*, Dutch Sheets calls us to the wall to stand guard and pray for the safety and preservation of our homes and our nation.
Bill Bright
Founder, Campus Crusade for Christ
Orlando, Florida

Watchman Prayer contains valuable lessons, stories and testimonies from around the world about how a people on the wall can watch and pray to impact cities, nations and, ultimately, the world.
Frank Damazio
Pastor, City Bible Church
Portland, Oregon

As the enemy of our souls roams the earth seeking whom he may devour, *Watchman Prayer* shows how the Body of Christ must exercise its God-given authority and stand on the wall and watch over our homes, our churches, our cities and our nations. Armed with the truth, our stand will be victorious!

Ted Haggard
Pastor, New Life Church
Colorado Springs, Colorado

A seasoned prayer leader who bounds after spiritual truth with the fervor of a bloodhound on the scent, Dutch Sheets hunts for insights whispered by the still, small voice of the Holy Spirit. In his quest he has captured unique truths about prayer, and he generously shares the feast with us in *Watchman Prayer*.

Jane Hansen
President/CEO, Aglow International
Edmonds, Washington

A prayer movement spreading all across the earth continues to gain momentum. Manifold insights are increasing as the Holy Spirit stirs each of us to responsiveness and responsibility. *Watchman Prayer* will help us answer to this moment.

Jack W. Hayford
Founding Pastor, The Church On The Way
President, The King's Seminary
Van Nuys, California

Watchman Prayer is a summons to all in the Body of Christ to take up positions as watchmen on the walls. Our families, our churches and the nations hang in the balance. This easy-to-read book expresses both the urgency we need in order to pray fervently and the encouragement we need to know that our ministry of intercession is making a difference.

Jim Hodges
President, Federation of Ministers and Churches
Duncanville, Texas

All across the earth, God is raising up men and women to watch over the nations, interceding for them in prayer. *Watchman Prayer* will give them the biblical understanding to effectually fulfill the mandate God has given them. A must-read for intercessors!

Cindy Jacobs
Cofounder, Generals of Intercession
Colorado Springs, Colorado

The church militant receives an up-to-date admonishing in *Watchman Prayer*. This warfare manual should be part of every believer's library. Read it and fight the good fight of faith.

Rev. Dean (Pappy) Sheets
Middletown, Ohio

Dutch Sheets has done it again! He has given us a book so practical and anointed that we are challenged to retreat to our favorite place of prayer and immediately apply these biblical principles—with every expectation of victory. A wonderful companion to *Intercessory Prayer*!

Quin Sherrer
Coauthor of *How to Pray for Your Children* and *Praying Prodigals Home*
Colorado Springs, Colorado

Keen observers tend to survive, as do companions of keen observers. Our spiritual survival often hangs by a slender thread, dependent on the eyesight and insight of watchmen on the walls. *Watchman Prayer* is like vitamin A for spiritual eyesight—an eye test for watchmen who, with shielded eyes, peer into the mist of eternity.

Dutch Sheets is a keen observer, a man who doesn't miss much, whether he's at a mall food court, at a deer stand in the forest or on his knees viewing eternity. He is one of a rare breed. He not only sees but can decipher what he sees. I feel safer knowing Dutch is out there watching . . . and training others to watch with him!

Tommy Tenney
Author of *The God Chasers* and *God's Dream Team*
Pineville, Louisiana

WATCHMAN PRAYER

DUTCH SHEETS

Regal

A Division of Gospel Light
Ventura, California, U.S.A.

Published by Regal Books
A Division of Gospel Light
Ventura, California, U.S.A.
Printed in U.S.A.

Regal Books is a ministry of Gospel Light, an evangelical Christian publisher dedicated to serving the local church. We believe God's vision for Gospel Light is to provide church leaders with biblical, user-friendly materials that will help them evangelize, disciple and minister to children, youth and families.

It is our prayer that this Regal book will help you discover biblical truth for your own life and help you meet the needs of others. May God richly bless you.

For a free catalog of resources from Regal Books/Gospel Light, please call your Christian supplier or contact us at 1-800-4-GOSPEL or www.regalbooks.com.

Cover Design by Barb Fisher
Interior Design by Debi Thayer
Edited by Wil Simon

Library of Congress Cataloging-in-Publication Data
Sheets, Dutch.
        Watchman prayer / Dutch Sheets.
            p. cm.
        Includes bibliographical references (p.).
        ISBN 0-8307-2567-9 (Hardcover)
        ISBN 0-8307-2568-7 (Paperback)
            1. Prayer–Christianity. 2. Spiritual warfare. I. Title.

    BV210.2 .S513 2000
    248.3'2–dc21
                                                                                00-039023
    1 2 3 4 5 6 7 8 9 10 11 12 13 14 15 / 07 06 05 04 03 02 01 00

Rights for publishing this book in other languages are contracted by Gospel Literature International (GLINT). GLINT also provides technical help for the adaptation, translation and publishing of Bible study resources and books in scores of languages worldwide. For further information, contact GLINT, P.O. Box 4060, Ontario, CA 91761-1003, U.S.A. You may also send e-mail to Glintint@aol.com, or visit their website at www.glint.org.

Contents

LOOKING FOR A FEW GOOD WATCHMEN

― Chapter One ―

BE CAREFUL WHAT YOU WATCH FOR

The only thing worse than shopping is watching someone shop. Except for my wife, of course. I don't mind at all following her around a mall for two or three hours. I show my interest periodically with pleasant little grunts—"Umph"; "Uh-huh"; "Ahh-hum." Sometimes I get downright wordy—"Yes"; "No"; "Sure"; "HOW MUCH!" I've gotten pretty quick at correcting that one, "Wow, what a deal!" I hastily add. About the closest thing I can compare "shopper watching" to would be watching a sewing match.

Which is why I'm sitting in the food court writing while my wife and youngest daughter, Hannah, shop. It's one of those outlet malls where they sell you the flawed stuff "on sale." My oldest daughter, Sarah, who is 10 years old, is with me, reading. She doesn't like shopping, either—yet. I informed her on the way to our "food court refuge" of the gene in her—which God gave all women—that simply hasn't kicked in yet. Told her not to worry, it'll happen.

[This was first written three years ago in my book *Intercessory Prayer*. Sarah is now 13 and her mother is proud to inform you that Sarah's shopping gene has fully kicked in. She is maturing nicely in this essential aspect of womanhood. I'm still eating in food courts—by myself now—and "umph"ing once in a while.]

In my studies of this genetic plague—most of them done through conversing with other men in food courts—I have discovered that no one knows for sure when the gene kicks in or what triggers it. It can hit anytime between the ages of 6 and 13. Sometimes it happens in the middle of the night; they just wake up with the shakes—flu-like symptoms. When it happened with Hannah, I was ready to anoint her with oil, until my wife, Ceci, informed me it wouldn't help.

"What do you mean it won't help?" I asked in surprise. "Of course it will."

"No," she said, "it's her shopping gene kicking in. We've got to get her to a mall—fast."

Mom was right, of course. She usually is. Hannah came home proudly holding her shopping bag, looking like she'd just caught her first fish. Women! Who can figure?

To prove my point, I just counted the men and women in the food court and surrounding stores—26 females and 9 males. Half the males were kids that had been dragged there against their wills. Another was writing—yours truly—and the rest were grunting, "Uh-huh." I felt sorry for one guy; he actually looked like a zombie. I think he finally cracked under the stress. Either that or he was suffering from food-court food poisoning.

Ceci and Hannah are back now, getting something to drink and showing us their "deals." I'm grunting. Ceci is merely dropping Hannah off so she can run back for one more thing. Seven-year-olds—apprentice shoppers—can't always keep up with the pros. They haven't had enough aerobics classes, for which the real motivation is shopping conditioning.

[Hannah is, of course, now 11, and her stamina is increasing regularly. Ceci assures me that she and Sarah are both right on schedule in this all important phase of development—she urged me "not to worry." The thought never crossed my mind!]

Why couldn't God have made women to like normal things, such as sitting in a woods for days in sub-zero weather, waiting for a deer or elk to walk by? Now that's my idea of exciting watching! . . . Or watching a football game! I'm not into TV too much—unless it's a good sporting event. Ceci doesn't always understand me in this area, but she is kind about it. "Who are you rooting for?" she sometimes asks.

"I don't care who wins," I often reply.

"Are these any of your favorite teams?"

"No, not really."

"A favorite player or two, perhaps?"

"Naw, I don't know much about these guys at all."

"Then why are you watching the game?" she asks with a quizzical expression.

"Because it's football," I reply as patiently as I possibly can. Sometimes people can't figure out the obvious. I'll tell you what puzzles me—why she and my two daughters like to watch stuff that makes them cry. Go figure!

Many kinds of watching take place: TV watching, parade watching, watching the clock, stock market watching, bird watching (ranks right up there with sewing matches to me) and a thousand other things. I like to watch kids laugh. I hate to watch people cry. I've watched individuals born; I've watched others die.

I once watched a lady in San Pedro, Guatemala, look for a watch. It was her husband's—he died in the earthquake of 1976. So did three of her kids. All she and her surviving infant had left were the clothes on their backs. Their small adobe home was a mound of dirt.

When our interpreter asked her what she was digging for, she replied. "A bag of beans we had and my husband's watch. He was sleeping about here when he was killed," she said, pointing at an area of approximately 10 square feet. "It would mean so much to me if I could find his watch."

We started digging.

Although it was like looking for a needle in a haystack, we asked God to help us and waded into the three-feet-deep dirt. Right then I'd have charged hell for that watch. We found it an hour or so later.

"Muchas gracias," she repeated through tears, as she clutched the inexpensive watch to her breast.

"Treasure" is such a relative term, I thought as I wiped my eyes. *I wish the world could see this. Maybe some priorities would change.*

I watched another quake victim, holding her three-year-old daughter, walk away from a food line in which I was serving. She was the last in line for the soup. As she held out the jar she had found, we looked at her and said, "No más" (which means "No more"). Then I watched her walk away, holding her hungry child.

Things got all messed up at that point in my life. Neat little lists of needs disappeared. Certain important goals became strangely irrelevant. Things that mattered suddenly didn't. Bank accounts were looked at differently, success was redefined. Funny how one glance into four eyes can bring such chaos. In many ways, order has never been restored.

Be careful what you watch.[1]

WATCHMEN NEED GOD'S 20/20 VISION

This introduction was taken from the final chapter of my first book, *Intercessory Prayer*. The chapter dealt with what I called the "watchman anointing." I want to pick up where I ended that book and develop fully the concept of the watchman. It is a facet of prayer being greatly emphasized by the Holy Spirit in this hour, and it *must* be understood.

God is certainly not finished with the prayer movement around the world. In fact, He wants to transform it from a "movement" to a lifestyle. Movements come and movements go; sometimes that's good and sometimes that's bad. Wouldn't it be sad if 20 years from now the prayer movement of the 1990s was only a "was," spoken of as the good old days!

Will our chapter of history be titled:

- Opportunities Left Unseized
- They Began Well, but . . .
- What Could Have Been?

I trust not. I hope our legacy is similar to King David's: He served God's purpose for his generation (see Acts 13:36). Or maybe like that of the Early Church: They turned their world upside down (see Acts 17:6, *AMP*).

If you're like me, I know you want to finish well. My hope is that prayer becomes the *lifestyle* of the Church and that the movement keeps moving until it takes root. By the grace and power of the Holy Spirit, we can make it so!

Yes, our history is yet to be written. Much is waiting for us: Testimonies are waiting to be created; a generation of youth is waiting to be born again; dry bones are waiting for breath (see Ezek. 37); homes are waiting to be healed; addictions are waiting to be broken; untold millions are waiting to hear the gospel for the first time.

Note some alarming statistics:

- In 1996, nearly 93,000 juveniles were charged in violent crimes—a number 60-percent higher than a decade ago.[2]
- A total of 5,000 young Americans kill themselves each year, making suicide the third highest cause of death among 15- to 24-year-olds. About 8 percent of teens have made a suicide attempt. Suicide rates for children and teens have quadrupled since 1950.[3]
- One million students grades 6-12 took a gun to school this year. Sixty-three percent of students who carried guns to school said they had threatened to harm another student.[4]
- In 1992, an estimated 2.9 million suspected child-abuse incidents were reported in the United States. An estimated 1,251 children were known to have died from child abuse. Those who survive often suffer long-lasting pain and even disability from serious injuries and emotional trauma.[5]
- Based on data on 15- to 19-year-old teens from the National Survey of Family Growth and the National Survey of Adolescent Males, recent research shows that 50 percent of female teens and 55 percent of male teens report they have had sexual intercourse at least once.[6]
- The ratio of abortions per live births remains at

roughly 25 percent. (In 1995-96, 26 percent of pregnancies ended in abortion.)[7]

- 1998 brought about no change in the percentage of adults who are born-again Christians.[8]
- When compared to statistics for 1991, church attendance and Bible reading are at lower levels of involvement.[9] (My note: This means we have actually lost ground.)
- Six out of 10 Americans (61 percent) agreed that "the Holy Spirit is a symbol of God's presence or power, but is not a living entity."[10]
- A majority of all born-again Christians also reject the existence of the Holy Spirit (55 percent).[11] (My note: These are of those who *profess* to be born again.)

We need a wake-up call. There simply is no hope for America apart from revival.

If watchmen had been on duty, these and other shocking events could have been averted. Satan takes advantage of us when the watchman concept of prayer is not operating, as is made clear in the following verse: "In order that no advantage be taken of us by Satan; for we are not ignorant of his schemes" (2 Cor. 2:11). The context is forgiveness, but a general principle is also revealed, which is very applicable to our subject. Let's analyze the verse more closely.

The word "ignorant" is from the Greek verb *agnoeo*, which means to be "without knowledge or understanding of."[12] Our English word "agnostic" is derived from it. Technically, an agnostic is not a person who is unsure if he or she believes in God, although we now use the word this way. In actuality, however, an agnostic is a person who does not know or understand, regardless of the subject. We also get the word "ignore" from the same root. In this verse we're urged not to ignore or be an agnostic—without understanding—where the devil is concerned.

"Schemes" is from the word *noema*, which literally means "thought." The verse is essentially saying, "Don't be without understanding of the way Satan thinks." *Noema* came to also mean "plans, schemes, plots, devices"[13] because these things are born in the thoughts of the mind. For greater insight, let's insert all these concepts into the verse: "Don't be without understanding of the way your enemy thinks and operates—of his plans, plots, schemes and devices." Is there not also a subtle promise here? If God suggests we are not to be ignorant of Satan's schemes, He must be willing to reveal them to us.

What if we are unaware of his schemes? He'll take advantage of us. The word "advantage" is derived from *pleonekteo*, which is a compound word meaning literally "to have or hold the greater portion" (*pleon*—"the greater part"; *echo*—"to have or hold").[14] It is easy to see why this is a word for "covet." It also means "overreach."[15]

In boxing, the person who has the longer reach has the advantage and usually gets in more blows. The word *pleonekteo* is also translated "make a gain"; Satan makes a lot of gains on those who are unaware of his ways. Bullinger says *pleonekteo* means "to make a prey of, to defraud."[16] Let's put all of these definitions together: "To the degree we are ignorant of the way our adversary thinks and operates—of his plans, plots, schemes and devices—to that degree he will gain on us, prey on us, defraud us of what is ours and have or hold the greater portion."

The greater portion of what? Whatever! Our homes, marriages, families, communities, money, government, nation and more. Twenty-five years ago the Church in America was without understanding of what Satan was planning, and he got the greater portion of our schools. The same could be said of our government and many of our churches!

Have you ever been taken advantage of? Have you ever received the smaller portion? In my Bible-college days we had a way of enlightening the superspiritual who thought it necessary to intercede for the world while giving thanks for a meal. They were *ignorant* of our *scheme* when we asked them to pray over the food. While they traversed the globe, we enjoyed *the greater portion* of their meals! It was a real test of their true spirituality. (I am deeply embarrassed by this abominable practice in my past and would never do it today. But for those of you who feel you must intercede over your food, save it for your prayer closet!)

Paul was taken advantage of in 1 Thessalonians 2:18. Satan gained on him (*pleonekteo*) in the ongoing war over spreading the gospel: "For we wanted to come to you—I, Paul, more than once—and yet Satan thwarted us." We know Paul won more battles than he lost. But he was human and at times Satan succeeded in thwarting his plans. Please notice it doesn't say God changed His mind about where Paul was to go. It clearly says that Satan hindered him. Those people who would have us think that Satan can do nothing except what God allows and that we are to ignore him, should reread these two verses. God doesn't ignore the devil and neither should we. And he certainly does a lot of things God doesn't *allow* him to do.

> Let's understand the ways of God and not credit Him for the results of our actions and Satan's. Let the responsibility fall where it should fall.

The only sense in which it can be said that God allows everything that happens on earth is that He created the laws and principles—sowing and reaping, cause and effect and the free will of humans—that govern the earth. We, however, implement these principles and determine much of what we reap and experience. It is truly God and humans working together. Satan, too, understands these laws and uses them to his advantage whenever possible.[17] Consider the following comments that reflect how easy it is for humans to blame God for failures, mishaps and consequences that are the result of human effort and Satan's role in human affairs:

- In *Christianity Today* Philip Yancey writes: "When Princess Diana died, I got a phone call from a television producer. 'Can you appear on our show?' he asked. 'We want you to explain how God could possibly allow such a terrible accident.'"
- At the 1994 Winter Olympics, when speed skater Dan Jansen's hand scraped the ice, causing him to lose the 500-meter race, his wife, Robin, cried out, "Why, God, again? God can't be that cruel!"
- A young woman wrote James Dobson this letter: "Four years ago, I was dating a man and became pregnant. I was so devastated! I asked God, 'Why have You allowed this to happen to me?'"
- In a professional bout, boxer Ray "Boom-Boom" Mancini slammed his Korean opponent with a hard right, causing a massive cerebral hemorrhage. At a press conference after the Korean's death, Mancini said, "Sometimes I wonder why God does the things he does."
- Susan Smith, who pushed her two sons in her car into a lake to drown and then blamed a black carjacker for the deed, wrote in her official confession: "I dropped to the lowest point when I allowed my children to go down that ramp into the water without me. I took off running and screaming, 'Oh God! Oh God, no! What have I done? Why did you let this happen?'"

• I once watched a television interview with a famous Hollywood actress whose lover had rolled off a yacht in a drunken stupor and drowned. The actress, who probably had not thought about God in months, looked at the camera, her lovely face contorted by grief, and asked, bizarrely, "How could a loving God let this happen?"[18]

Let's understand the ways of God and not credit Him for the results of our actions and Satan's. Let the responsibility fall where it should fall.

Two more verses give additional insight. The first is Ephesians 6:18: "With all prayer and petition pray at all times in the Spirit, and with this in view, *be on the alert* with all perseverance and petition for all the saints" (italics mine). The *King James Version* uses the word "watching" for the phrase "be on the alert."

The second verse is 1 Peter 5:8, "Be of sober spirit, *be on the alert*. Your adversary, the devil, prowls about like a roaring lion, seeking someone to devour" (italics mine). Again, other translations use the word "watchful." The context of both verses is spiritual warfare. Each mentions our adversary and challenges us to alertness or watchfulness, both for ourselves and for our brothers and sisters in Christ.

I want to draw four conclusions from these three verses— Ephesians 6:18, 1 Peter 5:8 and 2 Corinthians 2:11—as an introduction for our study of the watchman anointing:

1. *Protection from the attacks of our enemy—even for believers— is not automatic.* There is a part for us to play. Though God is sovereign, this does not mean He is literally in control of everything that happens. He has left much to the decisions and actions of humankind. If God

were going to protect or safeguard us from Satan's attacks regardless of what we did, these verses would be totally irrelevant to Christians. Somewhere in our theology, we must find a place for human responsibility. At some point we must begin to believe that we matter, that we're relevant, for ourselves and for others.

2. *God's plan is to warn or alert us to Satan's tactics.* This is deduced from the simple fact that, since God says not to be *unaware* of Satan's tactics, He must be willing to make us *aware* of them. If He says to be on the alert, this must mean that if we are, He will alert us. God wouldn't ask of us something He wasn't also going to enable us to accomplish.

3. *We must be alert—remain watchful—or we won't be aware of God's attempts to warn us of Satan's attacks and plans.* If these attacks were always going to be obvious, alertness wouldn't be necessary. Isaiah 56:10 speaks of blind watchmen. What a picture! I'm afraid it has been a fairly good description of many of us in our watching roles. We're often like the disciples of old: we have eyes, but we do not see (see Mark 8:18). It's time we do more than gaze; we must alertly watch!

4. *If we are not alert and watchful, if we are ignorant of Satan's schemes, he will take the bigger portion.* He will gain on us, taking advantage of our ignorance. Contrary to popular belief, we really can be destroyed due to ignorance (see Hosea 4:6). We may not like to admit it, but Satan really has gained a lot of territory in America.

We cannot deny the reality of spiritual conflict. If we do, we act in denial, and the results can be disastrous.

Don't be like the desert nomad who awakened hungrily one night and decided he'd have a midnight snack. Lighting a candle, he grabbed a date and took a bite. Holding the date to the candle, he saw a worm, whereupon he threw the date out of the tent. Biting into the second date, he found another worm and threw it away, also. Deciding he might not get anything to eat if this continued, he blew out the candle and ate the dates.[19]

Sometimes we, too, prefer the darkness of denial to the light of truth. Though the truth really does hurt at times, it is still truth. Denial doesn't change it. Where Satan has made gains, let's admit it and determine to take them back![20]

Watchmen Wanted

The first example of a failed watchman is recorded in the Bible and affects each one of us every day. The watchman's name was Adam. God told him in Genesis 2:15 to "keep" the garden. The word "keep" is the Hebrew word *shamar*, which is one of the three Old Testament words used for a watchman. I will define these three words in great depth over the next few chapters, but for now, suffice it to say, one of the main concepts of the word involves protection and preservation.

Adam was told to *protect* the garden, *watching* for attacks from the evil one, the serpent. Why do I assert this? Because first of all, it is much in keeping with the nature of God to have warned him. To have done otherwise would not have been consistent with God's character. Second, neither Adam nor Eve seemed shocked when a snake talked to them. It evidently didn't come as a total surprise. Third, what else could there have been before the Fall to guard, keep or protect themselves from in the garden? Only the serpent.[21] The first responsibility of watchmen is to keep the serpent out of their God-given gardens.

The serpent has been interloping ever since, seeking to grab the greater portion. He has sunk his venomous fangs into many portions of America and the world. The fruit of the poisonous venom is terrifying. Consider these reports concerning a young, identityless generation of Americans:

- A 1998 report shows that students aged 12-18 years were victims of about 255,000 incidents of nonfatal serious violent crime at school and about 671,000 incidents away from school.[22]
- On April 20, 1999, two young men wearing long, black trench coats opened fire in a suburban high school in Littleton, Colorado, injuring as many as 23 students and killing 12 students and one teacher, and then killed themselves.
- In June 1998, a male teacher and a female guidance counselor were shot in a hallway at a Richmond, Virginia, high school. The man suffered an injury to the abdomen that wasn't life threatening; the woman was reported as being grazed.
- In March 1998, four girls and a teacher were shot to death and 10 others were wounded during a false fire alarm at Westside Middle School in Jonesboro, Arkansas, when two boys, ages 11 and 13, opened fire from the woods. Both were convicted of murder in juvenile court and can be held up to the age of 21.
- In December 1997, three students were killed and five others wounded while they took part in a prayer circle in a hallway at Heath High School in West Paducah, Kentucky. A 14-year-old student pled guilty but

mentally ill to murder and is serving life in prison. One
of the wounded girls was left paralyzed.

• In October 1997, a 16-year-old outcast in Pearl, Mississippi, was accused of killing his mother and shooting nine students at Pearl High School. Two of them
died, including the suspect's ex-girlfriend. The 16-
year-old was sentenced to life in prison. Two others
went to trial on accessory charges.[23]

Our precious gardens are full of demons—we need some
watchmen!

Tragedies such as these can and must be eliminated. I challenge you to make a difference. Learn the power of prayer and
apply the principles of the watchman. We must take back the
portions Satan has seized in our nation and around the world.
Let's become spiritually militant and aggressive as we deal with
the serpent and his stealing, killing and destroying. Let there be
no more agnostics where Satan is concerned. Let's expose and
STOP HIM! Let's get him out of our gardens!

All across America thousands of youth are meeting in Torch
Grab rallies where they are encouraged to pick up the torch of
Columbine High School martyrs Cassie Bernall and Rachel
Scott. Many are responding with total commitment and aban-
donment to God, picking up the torch and accepting the call to
reach their generation for Christ.

The blood of these martyrs cries from the ground, "Revival
to this generation!" The same ears that heard the blood-cry of
righteous Abel hear those of righteous Cassie and Rachel. The
fire of the torches they carried is spreading to other torches
across this land. Once again, the blood of the martyrs will be the
seeds of revival.

What of us? What of we watchmen who are exhorted by God

to guard this generation and birth a revival? Must not our commitment match that of our fallen young comrades and their successors? Is this not a cause worth abandoning ourselves to? My good friend Solveig Henderson states it well for each of us. I pray you'll agree.

> *I'm abandoned to You, Jesus,*
> *I surrender to the call.*
> *I don't want to have my own way,*
> *'Cause I know through that I'll fall.*
> *So I come and fall on You, Lord.*
> *I will answer when You knock.*
> *When I'm weak You are my stronghold, my security,*
>   *my Rock.*

> *I'm abandoned to You, Jesus,*
> *You're the treasure that I seek.*
> *Anything that I've held sacred,*
> *By comparison is bleak.*
> *In my travels You're my journey,*
> *You're my road, my map, my guide.*
> *You're my final destination.*
> *I say yes.*[24]

The call goes out for watchman. Can you hear it? Surrender to the call!

Notes
1. Dutch Sheets, *Intercessory Prayer* (Ventura, CA: Regal Books, 1996), pp. 233-236.

2. Youth Culture Department, "Youth Culture Statistics," *Focus on the Family* (December 13, 1998), n.p., citing CNN Interactive, May 21, 1998.
3. Ibid., n.p., citing *Teen People* (November 1998), p. 70, and *USA Today* (August 13, 1998), n.p.
4. Youth Specialties, "Youth Culture Update," *Youthworker,* November/ December 1998. http://www.gospelcom.net/ys/free/stats (accessed April 2000), quoting *Time* and *USA Today* (June 29, 1998), n.p.
5. "Teens at Home" *Stop the Violence, Face the Music,* 2000. http://www.stv.net/contents/stats/05.html (accessed April 2000), quoting the National Committee for Prevention of Child Abuse, 1993.
6. U.S. Department of Health and Human Services, "A National Strategy to Prevent Teen Pregnancy, Annual Report 1997-98," *Office of the Assistant Secretary for Planning and Evaluation,* June 1998. http://aspe.hhs.gov/hsp/teenp/97-98rpt.htm (accessed September 22, 1999).
7. "Abortion's Unexpected Side Effects?" *Women's Wire,* 1999. http://www.women.com/news/forums/backtalk/E0819 (accessed September 22, 1999), quoting the Alan Guttmacher Institute.
8. "Annual Survey of America's Faith Shows No Significant Changes in Past Year," *Barna Research Online,* March 8, 1999. http://www.barna.org/cgi-bin/PagePressRelease.asp?PressReleaseID=17 (accessed April 2000).
9. "Christianity Showing No Visible Signs of a Nationwide Revival," *Barna Research Online,* March 3, 1998. http://www.barna.org/cgi-bin/PagePressRelease.asp?PressReleaseID=16 (accessed April 2000).
10. "Angels Are In—Devil and Holy Spirit Are Out," *Barna Research Online,* April 29, 1997. http://www.barna.org/cgi-bin/PagePressRelease.asp?PressReleaseID=3 (accessed April 2000).
11. Ibid.
12. Ethelbert W. Bullinger, *A Critical Lexicon and Concordance to the English and Greek New Testament* (Grand Rapids, MI: Zondervan Publishing House, 1975), p. 400.
13. Spiros Zodhiates, *Hebrew-Greek Key Study Bible—New American Standard,* rev. ed. (Chattanooga, TN: AMG Publishers, 1990), p. 1797.
14. Spiros Zodhiates, *The Complete Word Study Dictionary* (Iowa Falls, IA: Word Bible Publishers, 1992), p. 1173.
15. James Strong, *The New Strong's Exhaustive Concordance of the Bible* (Nashville, TN: Thomas Nelson Publishers, 1990), ref. no. 4122.
16. Bullinger, *Critical Lexicon and Concordance,* p. 28.
17. Sheets, *Intercessory Prayer,* pp. 138-140.

18. Craig Brian Larson, *Choice Contemporary Stories and Illustrations for Preachers, Teachers and Writers* (Grand Rapids, MI: Baker Book House, 1998), p. 28.

19. Craig Brian Larson, *Illustrations for Preaching and Teaching* (Grand Rapids, MI: Baker Book House, 1993), p. 59.

20. Sheets, *Intercessory Prayer*, pp. 237, 238.

21. Ibid., p. 244.

22. "Teens at School: Ten Years of School Violence," *Stop the Violence, Face the Music*, 2000. http://www.stv.net/contents/stats/04.html (accessed April 2000), quoting National Criminal Justice Reference Services, *Indicators of School Crime and Safety*, 1998, n.p.

23. "Teens at School: Ten Years of School Violence," *Stop the Violence, Face the Music*, 2000. http://www.stv.net/contents/stats/04.html (accessed April 2000).

24. Solveig and Ken Henderson, "Abandoned to You, Jesus" (n.p., n.d.). Used by permission.

GOD'S ALARM SYSTEM

Chapter Two

THE BIG PICTURE ON GOD'S WATCHMEN

We recently built a new, custom home—and I'm still saved. This is due much more to the grace of God and a detailed wife than anything else. From overruns to misunderstood instructions to contractor delays, there were plenty of opportunities to lose it when we were building our home. Thank God for a detail-oriented wife who did most of our work, a good Christian builder who walks in integrity and the grace of God.

When beginning the project, we started with the big picture and then worked our way down to the details. I was more involved in the big picture, thank goodness. I'm a big picture, bottom-line, "don't bore me with the details" kind of guy.

"What's it gonna look like?" and "How much will it cost?" were about as deep as my questions got.

When I share my bright ideas and lofty visions, Ceci always wants to talk details: "What about this?" "Have you thought of that?" "Who is going to do this and such?"

"That's for someone else to worry about," I quickly and impatiently respond. "I have a dream. Don't bother me with all that stuff."

It really doesn't matter to me that "all that stuff" will no doubt make or break the project. Thinking about all that stuff would break *me*—raise my blood pressure and give me stress. So I don't administrate. I leave that for the weird people God made with abnormal desires.

I have a friend, Randall Gant, who told me the other day he actually loves to solve problems. I'm afraid this dear brother has a problem someone needs to help *him* solve. He told me he woke up the other day thinking about a flow chart. He was serious! I was ready to pray for him; he, on the other hand, was excited. He thinks God made him this way. My theology won't let me believe God is that cruel. People like him weren't born this way—they probably did something really bad as children and this is their punishment.

What does all that have to do with this book? Not much—I just needed to get it off my chest! But there is some relevance. In this chapter we're going to look at the big picture where watchmen are concerned: the broad concepts and definitions as opposed to specific principles and how-tos. In subsequent chapters we'll get to some details—God have mercy on my soon-to-be-troubled soul!

So, for you detail people . . . chill! We'll make you happy later.

For you big picture people . . . enjoy! Relax! Indulge yourself! Dream a little.

The Role of Watchmen

Those of you who have read my book *Intercessory Prayer* (in other words, the most spiritual of you!) will recall that I sometimes refer to spiritual abilities and activities as anointings. This is simply because anything we accomplish of eternal value is brought about by the ability and empowerment of the Holy Spirit. Through anointings of the Holy Spirit, Jesus preached, liberated spiritual captives, healed people and did other good works (see Luke 4:18-19; Acts 10:38). In the Old Testament, kings were anointed to rule and priests were anointed to serve and to minister. For us as well, it is the anointing of the Holy Spirit that enables us to adequately perform spiritual activities.

In this book I use the phrase "watchman anointing." This is not done to imply that only a select few with unique callings can operate in this type of prayer activity. Nor is it insinuating that we wait on some heavenly visitation before moving into this type of prayer. It is simply a way of stating and reminding us that the Holy Spirit will empower us and give us the ability to function in this wonderful ministry.

The three primary Hebrew words in the Old Testament for watchman are *natsar, shamar* and *tsaphah*. These words have both a defensive or protective connotation and an offensive or aggressive application, with the defensive aspect being the most prominent in the Scriptures. We will discuss the defensive meanings in these next chapters, then later examine the offensive aspect.

Combining the definitions of these three words, which are used almost synonymously, their defensive concept essentially means *to guard or protect through watching over or concealing*. While applied to many subjects—crops, people, cities, etc.—the concept is usually *preservation*.

The two New Testament Greek words for "watching," *gregoreuo* and *agrupneo*, also refer to protection but they have the literal meanings of "being awake" or "sleepless." The picture is that of a sentry, lookout or night watchman who is supposed to remain awake and alert, watching for signs of trouble. Hence the translation at times "be on the alert" (see Luke 21:36, 1 Cor. 16:13, Eph. 6:18, 1 Pet. 5:8).

As He does so often in Scripture, the Holy Spirit uses these practical, physical activities of watchmen to symbolize spiritual functions, usually in reference to prophetic warnings and intercessory prayer.

Watching for Wolves, Thieves and Enemy Assaults

Let's broaden our understanding of biblical watchman by looking at the two most prominent contextual usages of the word in the Old Testament:

• Watching over and protecting crops
• Watchmen on the walls of cities

First, those who watched crops were stationed on rocks, buildings or towers to provide a better range of vision. Towers or outposts in the fields usually had sleeping quarters because it was necessary to keep watch day and night during harvest. The watchmen would take shifts—one working, one sleeping—and thereby "watch" 24 hours a day.

This has great symbolism for us. Seasons of harvest necessitate a more urgent need for watchmen, as the "thief" (see John 10:10) is going to do all he can to steal the harvest and keep the greater portion. It is little wonder that God has preceded the greatest harvest of souls the world has ever known—which is now happening—with the greatest prayer awakening in history. The Lord of the harvest is wise. I can assure you He has 24-hour sentries watching the harvest. May we be able to say with our Lord, "Of those You have given me, not one of them perished" (see John 17:12).

Paul and Silas were in danger of losing a very significant harvest in Acts 16. They had been supernaturally led westward into Europe with the message of Christ and had witnessed the first European convert, Lydia (see Acts 16:6-15). At this time a girl with a spirit of divination (Greek: *puthon*—python)[1] began to follow Paul and Silas saying, "These men are bond-servants of the Most High God, who are proclaiming to you the way of salvation" (v. 17).

Paul, discerning by the Holy Spirit her demonization, turned and commanded the spirit to leave her; and she was instantly delivered. Had Paul not discerned by the Spirit this girl's true condition, but accepted her endorsement, it could have seriously damaged his credibility. At the very least it may have allowed a mixture into this newborn Church, creating the delusion that Christianity and divination were compatible.

This point is also made by Gordon Lindsay in his commentary on Acts:

Satan is clever in his relentless war against God and His people. The evil spirit, of course, immediately recognized Paul and his party as bearers of the true message of God, and it might have denounced them vehemently. But a different strategy was adopted by Satan, who no doubt was following the party's fortunes with malevolent interest. Why not identify the religion of the oracles with that of Christianity? This would confuse and mislead the people so they would not understand that Christianity

had no relation whatever with the heathen gods of
Greece.[2]

Peter Wagner points out that Satan's strategy failed and
instead worked toward the prospering of the gospel:

This episode of strategic-level spiritual warfare would
affect the whole city of Philippi. Therefore, the more
public the battle the better. If Paul had cast out the
Python spirit the first day, few would have known about
it. But when it finally happened, it turned out to be a
major public display of the power of God over the power
of Satan, and the territorial spirit over Philippi was thoroughly embarrassed. The strongman had been bound in
the name of Jesus. The way had been opened for
the gospel to spread and for a powerful church to be
planted.[3]

Because of Paul's ability to discern and deal with the serpent's subtle attempt to steal the early harvest in Europe, a great
church was planted at Philippi. Remember the first responsibility of watchmen, as seen from Adam's assignment to keep or
protect the garden, is to keep the serpent out. Paul did this in
Philippi. (Isn't it interesting that the spirit's name was that of a
serpent?)

Secondly, watchmen were also posted on the city walls usually near the gates, where they functioned as sentries. This is
described in the following Old Testament references:

For thus the Lord says to me, "Go, station the lookout,
let him report what he sees. When he sees riders, horse-
men in pairs, a train of donkeys, a train of camels, let

him pay close attention, very close attention." Then the lookout called, "O Lord, I stand continually by day on the watchtower, and I am stationed every night at my guard post" (Isa. 21:6-8).

Lift up a signal against the walls of Babylon; post a strong guard, station sentries, place men in ambush! For the LORD has both purposed and performed what He spoke concerning the inhabitants of Babylon (Jer. 51:12).

On your walls, O Jerusalem, I have appointed watchmen; all day and all night they will never keep silent. You who remind the LORD, take no rest for yourselves (Isa. 62:6).

From the walls of the cities, they watched for two things: messengers and enemies. Their purpose in watching for messengers was to inform the gatekeepers when to open the gates and when to keep them closed. In those days runners were used to carry messages from city to city, and the watchmen would cry out when a messenger was coming. Skilled watchmen could sometimes even recognize the runners "by their stride" before ever seeing their faces. In 2 Samuel 18:27 the watchman said, "The running... is like the running of Ahimaaz." Do you see any important symbolism here?

Seasoned watchmen are often alerted by the Holy Spirit, before ever having any concrete evidence, that certain messengers are not to be trusted. They recognize wolves sent to devour the flock, or hirelings with improper motives, and bring warnings to those in leadership. Being alerted by their stride—something just doesn't seem right—watchmen sense and discern. To be sure, we must guard against human suspicion and judging after the flesh. But I have learned to listen to my trusted watchmen (one of whom is my wife) when uneasiness prevails about so and so. They are usually right. At times, these watchmen are unable to give me specific reasons, which is difficult for my analytical mind, but I have learned to trust them.

In *The New Yorker* (5/15/95), Sara Mosle recounts:

On March 18, 1937, a spark ignited a cloud of natural gas that had accumulated in the basement of the London, Texas, school. The blast killed 293 people, most of them children. The explosion happened because the local school board wanted to cut heating costs. Natural gas, the by-product of petroleum extraction, was siphoned from a neighboring oil company's pipeline to fuel the building's furnace free of charge. London never recovered from the blast that turned the phrase "boom town" into a bitter joke. The one positive effect of this disastrous event was government regulation requiring companies to add an odorant to natural gas. The distinctive aroma is now so familiar that we often forget natural gas is naturally odorless.[4]

Many of Satan's activities are "odorless"—hidden from our natural senses. God has added odorants to the evil one's works, however, that can be discerned by spiritual senses. Hebrews 5:14 tells us, "But solid food is for the mature, who because of practice have their senses trained to discern good and evil." Most false doctrine, division and general destruction in the Body of Christ could be averted if the watchmen would exercise these senses and the leaders would listen! Peter speaks of this need in 2 Peter 2:1,2:

But false prophets also arose among the people, just as there will also be false teachers among you, who will secretly introduce destructive heresies, even denying the Master who bought them, bringing swift destruction upon themselves. And many will follow their sensuality, and because of them the way of the truth will be maligned.

Paul warned the Ephesians of it in Acts 20:28-31:

Be on guard for yourselves and for all the flock, among which the Holy Spirit has made you overseers, to shepherd the church of God which He purchased with His own blood. I know that after my departure savage wolves will come in among you, not sparing the flock; and from among your own selves men will arise, speaking perverse things, to draw away the disciples after them. Therefore be on the alert, remembering that night and day for a period of three years I did not cease to admonish each one with tears.

> When the watchmen are functioning properly, we need never be caught off guard by Satan and his forces.

Evidently these Ephesians heeded Paul's advice for the Lord commended them in Revelation 2:2 (italics mine):

I know your deeds and your toil and perseverance, and that you cannot endure evil men, and *you put to the test those who call themselves apostles, and they are not, and you found them to be false.*

The watchmen on the wall also looked for enemies. When they saw potential danger approaching, they sounded an alarm, either by a shout or with a trumpet blast. Soldiers could then prepare themselves for battle and defend the city. Watchmen do this today, in a spiritual sense. They alert the Body of Christ to attacks of the enemy, sounding the alarm. When the watchmen are functioning properly, we need never be caught *off guard* by Satan and his forces. This may seem somewhat idealistic, but I'm convinced of its truth. I don't believe God ever intends for Satan to "take advantage" or get the bigger portion (see 2 Cor. 2:11). The famed "Dutch evangelist Corrie ten Boom was right to observe: 'It's a poor soldier indeed who does not recognize the enemy.' The key to victory in both natural and spiritual warfare is to clearly identify the enemy, and to understand his character and methods."[5]

As watchmen we do not live in fear of our adversary, nor do we live in ignorance of him. Contrary to what some would teach, alertness and vigilance are not synonymous with preoccupation. I must warn you, it is a common tactic of the enemy to dissuade Christians from watching for him by accusing them of a wrong emphasis.

Sadly enough, this message is often purported by well-meaning Christians. They teach that Satan is to be ignored or that little attention is to be paid him. No passage in the Bible supports this. Certainly we are not to become infatuated with Satan, but a good soldier is a well-informed soldier concerning his enemy. Be infatuated with and in awe of Jesus—be aware of the enemy. Love worship, not warfare; but when necessary, go to war. And post the sentries!

A classic story that stresses the importance of being vigilant was seen in the conflict between the Arabs and Turks in the early part of this century:

Aqaba in 1917 seemed impregnable. Any enemy vessel approaching the port would have to face the battery of huge naval guns above the town. Behind Aqaba in every direction lay barren, waterless, inhospitable desert. To the east lay the deadly "anvil of the sun." The Turks believed Aqaba to be safe from any attack. But they were wrong.

Lawrence of Arabia led a force of irregular Arab cavalry across the "anvil of the sun." Together, they rallied support among the local people. On July 6, 1917, the Arab forces swept into Aqaba from the north, from the blind side. A climactic moment of the magnificent film Lawrence of Arabia is the long, panning shot of the Arabs on their camels and horses, with Lawrence at their head, galloping past the gigantic naval guns that are completely powerless to stop them. The guns were facing in the wrong direction. Aqaba fell, and the Turkish hold on Palestine was broken, to be replaced by the British mandate and eventually by the State of Israel.

The Turks failed to defend Aqaba because they made two mistakes. They did not know their enemy, and they did not have the right weapons.

We must be careful not to make the same mistakes, Ephesians 6:12 makes it very clear who our enemy is: "Our struggle is not against flesh and blood, but against the rulers, against the authorities, against the powers of this dark world."[6]

We, too, must be aware of our enemy. Do we major on Satan or his demons? No, but we must discern their activities and, unlike these Turks, never walk in ignorance.

We are watchmen warriors who neither emphasize nor ignore the devil. We follow our loving Savior while remembering that He is also a mighty warrior. Through Him we are more than conquerors!

The Many Kinds of Watchmen Today

Before we move on to the next chapter and look at more specific definitions and applications of the watchman anointing, this is a good place to comment on the various realms of calling as watchmen. The anointing and responsibility to function in this needed activity can range from doing it for an individual person or home to watching for a nation or nations.

Cindy Jacobs of Generals of Intercession and Dr. C. Peter Wagner of Global Harvest Ministries are certainly watchmen for nations. While ministering abroad, it is not uncommon for them to receive insight and direction that, when acted on and prayed over properly, has significant impact on the particular nation involved.

Cindy Jacobs tells of how the Lord powerfully impacted the nation of Argentina as she and other intercessors sought His strategy for that nation. As they prayed for wisdom and insight, the Lord revealed various strongholds that needed to be dealt with and directed them to pray at the Plaza Mayo in Buenos Aires. The significance of this location was emphasized as they realized this plaza was surrounded by several buildings representing each of the strongholds that needed prayer. As Cindy led the prayer team from one building to the next, the Lord directed them specifically how to pray regarding each stronghold. They asked God to come heal and restore this nation.

The remarkable changes in Argentina since that time of prayer have been amazing! The run-down plaza has been restored from the ground up. The Argentine Agriculture Department issued a report that the land suddenly began to produce for no known reason; the fertility of the land increased without receiving any improvements. The Congress gave hectares of land to the native peoples as restitution. The inflation rate dropped from 3,000 percent to 1.5 percent. The *Wall Street Journal* reported, "There is a revival in the economy of Argentina, but nobody knows why." History indeed belongs to the watchman intercessor![7]

Peter Wagner, though in a totally different manifestation of the watchman anointing, seems to have incredible insight as to trends and themes the Holy Spirit is emphasizing to the Church around the world. As would a watchman on the wall of a city waiting for messengers, he alerts the Body of Christ to the message of the Spirit. The recent prayer movement is a prime example, and Peter has been one of its leading voices. Though particularly impacting America, it has also had a profound impact on other nations.

In 1997 the Lord instructed Peter and his wife, Doris, to take a prayer journey to Turkey. While debriefing at home later about Turkey, "Operation Queen's Palace" was born—a strategy to have teams of intercessors from the nations of the world participate in a massive prayer initiative. As Turkey and Ephesus are included in both the 10/40 Window and the 40/70 Window, Turkey appears to be the principal hinge nation for this area of the world. It is also the recognized spawning grounds for worldwide goddess worship. The Queen of Heaven (Operation "Queen's" Palace) is considered a chief principality commissioned by Satan to keep unbelievers in spiritual darkness. She is at the spiritual roots of Islam, with ancient Ephesus as one of her principal power centers.

Operation Queen's Palace was undoubtedly one of the most significant actions ever taken to push back the forces of darkness so that the light of the gospel can penetrate the hearts of unbelievers blinded to the love of Jesus Christ. Multiple prophetic prayer initiatives were held throughout the world, specifically targeted against every known manifestation of the power of the Queen of Heaven. Operation Queen's Palace culminated at Celebration Ephesus on October 1, 1999, where over 5,000 people gathered in the ancient Ephesian amphitheater to worship the Lord Jesus Christ and declare the Word of God for over four hours. Undoubtedly, the impact of these events will continue to reverberate throughout the nations of the world, as the strongholds of Satan are broken and multitudes come into the kingdom of God.[8]

Other individuals seem to have more of a calling as watchmen to a particular nation. Although he also ministers internationally, Chuck Pierce of Glory of Zion is a watchman I believe fits this description. He frequently has prophetic insight for all or part of America, which helps to thwart the powers of darkness and release the kingdom of God. I would not presume to define his calling for him—perhaps he is an international watchman as well—but my observations of his ministry have been limited to the United States.

The Holy Spirit frequently gives Chuck Pierce specific insight as to what needs to be done and how to pray concerning certain regions of the United States. When obeyed, breakthroughs always follow. Barbara Wentroble shares one of these experiences in her book *Prophetic Intercession*:

I remember a prophecy told to me in 1994 by Chuck Pierce. He had just returned from speaking at a meeting in Houston. While ministering, the Lord gave him a vision and spoke a prophetic word through him. The word from the Lord said that the next 24 days would be critical. God was looking at Houston and would break structures that were holding back revelation. He said the revelation would be released like rain. The prophecy continued to say that as the people looked, a river would begin to rise in the east. A literal fire would be on the river and come to the city. There was instruction for intercessors to gather together and pray during the night. The prayers would limit the destruction that would come to the area.

God was calling intercessors to pray for 24 days. Deborah DeGar, an intercessor from the Houston area, alerted local churches. She also led a prayer meeting from 3:00 A.M. to 6:00 A.M. during those 24 days. Exactly 24 days later, Houston experienced one of the worst floods recorded in the history of the city. The San Jacinto River, east of the city, flooded throughout Houston. A gas line broke and caused a literal fire on the river. As a result of the prophetic warning followed by the fulfillment of the prophetic word, the city experienced a new move of the Holy Spirit.[9]

This is a clear example of a watchman issuing a warning to a city, and watchmen intercessors responding properly.

A friend of mine, whom we'll call Margie, is another example of a watchman for a nation. At the age of 12, the Lord called her to pray for America and told her she would one day live in Washington, DC. She moved there in 1974, and her call to intercession increased in 1976. Still serving today in our nation's capital, she continues to be devoted to daily intercession for America. Margie has helped coordinate dozens of prayer excursions on and around Capitol Hill. God has given her great favor with church and government leaders alike. She has personally met with many members of Congress to pray for them and to offer biblical counsel.

Because of her long tenure of prayer in DC, Margie has a tremendous authority there in the Spirit, as well as very keen discernment. Our church, Springs Harvest Fellowship, has relied on her expertise on several occasions, allowing her to set the prayer agenda for prayer teams we send to Washington, DC.

Just a few months ago, the Lord gave her five specific reasons why the prayer team we were sending at that time should focus on the financial arena of our nation. She and the team sought the Lord for spiritual insight, specific words, proclamations and prophetic acts, and also received briefings from knowledgeable people regarding several strategic places. As God uncovered hidden information, the Holy Spirit alerted them to the seriousness of the situation. They followed the Lord's directives and spent several days praying specifically in various locations. Almost immediately, significant events began to take place. We believe God will continue to move in this area as a result of these watching prayers over this realm of our nation.

Watchmen are also assigned to other geographical areas, such as specific regions, states, cities and even neighborhoods. The United States Spiritual Warfare Network now has individuals coordinating intercession for all 50 states. They're watchmen for their individual states and coordinate other intercessors who watch smaller regions. God is literally blanketing America with prayer. The results will be increased harvest and ultimately revival. For example:

When intercessors in Texas became aware of an upcoming vote in Willow Park, they took their places as watchmen for that area. The county had been a dry county for years, meaning that liquor-by-the-drink was not allowed. No beer was sold at the grocery stores and there weren't any bars. In Willow Park's upcoming election some groups were trying to pass a liquor-by-the-drink law. Not wanting the atmosphere that would come with the bars and liquor sales to infiltrate their community, these watchmen prayed and fasted for three days. They prayed against the bondage of addiction and that people would come out to vote against the proposal. It came as no surprise that this law was defeated by a landslide. When God establishes His watchmen to pray His will, He will hear their prayers.[10]

There are also watchmen assigned to churches, individuals and, of course, families. These roles will be discussed in detail later in the book. Each of us should be involved in those realms of watching intercession. As we do so more faithfully and effectively, much will change.

Let's find our place on the wall, watchmen. *San Francisco Chronicle* columnist Herb Caen writes, "Every morning in Africa, a gazelle wakes up. It knows it must run faster than the fastest lion or it will be killed. Every morning a lion wakes up. It knows it must outrun the slowest gazelle or it will starve to death. It doesn't matter whether you are a lion or a gazelle; when the sun comes up, you'd better be running."[11]

Let's run the race on our knees!

Notes

1. James Strong, *The New Strong's Exhaustive Concordance of the Bible* (Nashville, TN: Thomas Nelson Publishers, 1990), ref. no. 4436.
2. Gordon Lindsay, *Acts in Action*, vol. 3 (Dallas, TX: Christ For The Nations, 1975), p. 93.
3. C. Peter Wagner, *Blazing the Way* (Ventura, CA: Regal Books, 1995), p. 76.
4. Edward K. Rowell, *Fresh Illustrations for Preaching and Teaching* (Grand

Rapids, MI: Baker Book House, 1997), p. 103.

5. Corrie ten Boom, quoted in Elizabeth Alves, *Becoming a Prayer Warrior* (Ventura, CA: Renew Books, 1998), p. 97.

6. Rowell, *Fresh Illustrations for Preaching and Teaching,* p. 195.

7. Cindy Jacobs, "Healing and Deliverance Through Spiritual Warfare for the Nations," comp., John Sandford, *Healing the Nations* (Grand Rapids, MI: Chosen Books, 2000), pp. 202-212.

8. C. Peter Wagner, "Operation Queen's Palace—A Proposal for a Major International Prayer Journey and Prophetic Act" (paper for Global Harvest Ministries, Colorado Springs, CO, January 1998), n.p. See also "Celebration Ephesus News Release" issued by the World Prayer Center, Colorado Springs, CO, October 5, 1999.

9. Barbara Wentroble, *Prophetic Intercession* (Ventura, CA: Renew Books, 1999), p. 38.

10. Cindy Jacobs, *Possessing the Gates of the Enemy* (Tarrytown, NY: Chosen Books, 1991), pp. 59, 60.

11. Craig Brian Larson, *Illustrations for Preaching and Teaching* (Grand Rapids, MI: Baker Book House, 1993), p. 216.

LISTEN SLOWLY

Chapter Three

GOD IS ALL EARS

I love hanging out in the woods. I like the solitude, but I also enjoy watching the animals. I've observed birds, squirrels, rabbits, coyotes, deer, elk, antelope and probably a dozen or so other creatures in the wild. Once in a while I love to sit still enough for them to get close, and then I make them aware of my presence by moving slightly or making some sort of noise.

When wild animals hear something or someone, they suddenly come to *attention* and are "all ears." Their ears prick up, listening intently for the slightest sound, as they know their very lives may depend on how well they listen. They have learned to *pay attention*.

The Hebrew word *qashab* describes this sort of alertness. Zodhiates defines it as "to prick up the ears, i.e., sharpening them like an alert animal; *to pay attention* (italics mine)."[1] Whether observing a domesticated animal or one in the wild, I'm sure most of you have witnessed this twitching or pricking of the ears when an animal comes to *attention*.

God does this. I'm not implying His ears twitch or prick up, but this pictorial word, *qashab*, is used to describe His *attention's* being captured by His children talking to Him. Psalm 66:19 refers to this: "But certainly God has heard; He has *given heed* to the voice of my prayer" (italics mine). Several other verses in the Psalms and elsewhere also use *qashab* to describe the Father's *attentive* listening to our prayers (see Ps. 17:1; 55:2; 61:1; 86:6; 130:2; and 142:6).

In the same way that His eyes roam to and fro throughout the earth, seeking those whose hearts are truly His (see 2 Chron. 16:9), His ears are always listening for the voices of His children. When He hears us, our words capture His *attention* like an animal's coming to alertness—He is all ears. He loves us so much!

In his book *Stress Fractures*, Charles Swindoll writes:

I vividly remember some time back being caught in the undertow of too many commitments in too few days. It wasn't long before I was snapping at my wife and our children, choking down my food at mealtimes, and feeling irritated at those unexpected interruptions through the day. Before long, things around our home started reflecting the pattern of my hurry-up style. It was becoming unbearable.

I distinctly recall after supper one evening the words of our younger daughter, Colleen. She wanted to tell me about something important that had happened to her at school that day. She hurriedly began, "Daddy-I-wanna-tell-you-somethin'-and-I'll-tell-you-really-fast."

Suddenly realizing her frustration, I answered, "Honey, you can tell me . . . and you don't have to tell me really fast. Say it slowly."

I'll never forget her answer: "Then listen slowly."[2]

You'll never find yourself having to say to your heavenly Father, "Then listen slowly." He has all the time in the world where you are concerned.

My secretary, Joy Anderson, tells of a similar, humorous family story:

While my sister-in-law was busy in the kitchen preparing dinner and planning for various family and church activities, her young daughter continued to talk to her about many different important things in her life, to which her mother would periodically respond, "Uh-huh." Finally, wanting to do something to make this more of a two-sided conversation, the little girl tugged on her mother's arm to get her full *attention*. Once she knew her mother was really listening to her, she said, "Mom, why don't you talk for awhile now, and I'll say 'Uh-huh.'"

I want to say this to you—God is never so preoccupied that He isn't really listening to you. You'll never find Him so involved with someone else, or so intent on running the universe, that He feigns *attentiveness* to you, mumbling "Uh-huhs," while actually thinking about something else. He can't wait to visit with you!

Pay Close Attention

Psalm 34:15 combines both the *attentive* eyes and the *attentive* ears into one verse, "The eyes of the LORD are toward the righteous, and His ears are open to their cry." The Psalmist goes on to say in verse 17, "The righteous cry, and the Lord hears and delivers them out of all their troubles." "Hears" in verse 17, though translated from a different Hebrew word, *shama*, is just as meaningful: "to hear intelligently with *attention*; to eavesdrop. The main idea is perceiving a message or sensing a sound."[3] Zodhiates goes on to say that *shama* is a synonym of *qashab*.

God is eavesdropping on us, waiting for us to speak a few words to Him. I love that! He just can't wait to visit with His kids. And when we do talk to Him, He gives great *attention* to what we're saying. His eavesdropping certainly isn't from the legalistic perspective some seem to believe of Him. God isn't sitting in heaven with His rod of discipline or scorebook, just waiting for us to make a mistake or say something wrong. He is listening because He so loves to communicate with us.

A picture of God's heart toward us and our inability to comprehend can be seen in the story of the boy who thought he was going to be shot. "Belden C. Lane writes in the *Christian Century* about English raconteur T. H. White, who recalls in *The Book of Merlyn* a boyhood experience. 'My father made me a wooden castle big enough to get into, and he fixed real pistol barrels beneath its battlements to fire a salute on my birthday, but made me sit in front the first night . . . to receive the salute, and I, believing I was to be shot, cried.'"[4]

So many people do not understand God's heart toward His kids. He is waiting, longing for a visit; they are waiting to be "shot." Controlled by our own fears and distorted perceptions of who God really is, we rob ourselves and Him of the pleasure He intended for the relationship.

Malachi 3:16 is another verse that uses the word *qashab* to describe the Father's careful *attention* toward us: "Then those who feared the Lord spoke to one another, and the Lord gave *attention* and heard it, and a book of remembrance was written before Him for those who fear the Lord and who esteem His name" (italics mine).

The context of this verse is God's pronouncing judgment due to rebellion and apostasy. Does a serious and important activity such as this keep Him from hearing His own and listening to them? No way! His compassion and relational desires toward us are never outweighed by wrath and the judgment of His enemies.

As absolutely thrilling as this is, it is only half of the needed understanding for watchmen. Our *attentiveness* to the Father is equally as important as the Father's *attentiveness* to us. The same word, *qashab,* is also used to describe our intent listening to God (see Prov. 4:20-22; 5:1; 7:24). The pricking of an animal's ears should also be descriptive of our intense desire to listen for the voice of our Father.

This kind of attentiveness is crucial for a proper functioning as a watchman. In this and the next two chapters, we will mention no less than 18 different ways the three Hebrew and two Greek words for watchman or watching are translated in the Scriptures. Each concept will give us different insights into what it means to be a watchman. Can you guess what the first translation is? It is: "PAY ATTENTION!"

Listen for Him—He's listening for you. It is important to recognize that there are different degrees of listening. In Matthew 11:15, Jesus said, "He who has ears to hear, let him hear." In other words, some were listening to Him without really hearing.

Do You Hear What I Hear?

Several years ago, my daughter Hannah was on my lap while I

was engrossed in something very important on TV—I think it was a football game. She, only three or four years old at the time, of course wasn't interested in the game. (For some weird reason, she, like most girls her age, still isn't very interested in football.)

As children do, *especially girls,* she was jabbering incessantly. Between first downs and touchdowns I was uh-huhing and nodding. Finally, she took her two small index fingers, placed them on my cheeks, turned my face toward hers and teasingly said, "Dad, look me in the eyes and listen to me."

Women are taught these things at a young age!

For those of you now burdened for me and planning to send me articles from Dr. Dobson on child rearing, please don't! This was a humorous occasion—Hannah and I enjoyed a good laugh. Please be assured that we do have serious and uninterrupted conversations, giving full *attention* to each other.

Tim Hansel in *When I Relax I Feel Guilty* points out the different levels of listening with the following story:

An American Indian was in downtown New York, walking with his friend who lived in New York City. Suddenly he said, "I hear a cricket."

"Oh, you're crazy," his friend replied.

"No, I hear a cricket. I do! I'm sure of it."

"It's the noon hour. There are people bustling around, cars honking, taxis squealing, noises from the city. I'm sure you can't hear it."

"I'm sure I do." He listened *attentively* and then walked to the corner, across the street, and looked all around. Finally on the corner he found a shrub in a large cement planter. He dug beneath the leaves and found a cricket. His friend was astounded. But the Cherokee said, "No. My ears are no different from yours. It simply depends on what you are listening to. Here, let me show you." He reached into his pocket and pulled out a handful of change—a few quarters, some dimes, nickels and pennies. And he dropped it on the concrete. Every head within a block turned. "You see what I mean?" he said as he began picking up his coins. "It all depends on what you are listening for."[5]

It isn't that God so rarely speaks. I believe we're not hearing Him because we listen so infrequently and have not trained ourselves to hear His voice.

When Ceci asks me, "What did I just say?" I immediately start squirming. She knows I wasn't really hearing her. I usually apologize with a "Sorry, God was telling me something" or some similar lie. (Not really—lighten up!)

In her book *Becoming a Prayer Warrior,* Beth Alves shares the following important wisdom on being *attentive* to the Lord:

Many times you and I don't hear God's directive because we have not inclined our ear to Him. The prerequisite to hearing is listening! Often we are so busy talking ourselves that we can't possibly hear Him. And yet, He wants us to be so attuned to His voice that we can even hear Him in the midst of a crowd. Someone has said that we have one mouth and two ears because we need to listen twice as much as we speak.

And as we listen, we find that God's tone of voice changes just like ours does. Sometimes the Lord speaks with a loud thunder; other times He speaks in a still small voice. The Word commands us to keep on the alert; keep watching and waiting. When He calls us to intercede for someone, the Holy Spirit will reveal strongholds, special burdens, battle plans of the enemy, actions to take and prayer strategies. We must learn to identify His voice and to be sensitive to responding quickly. Remember listening gets better as intimacy deepens.[6]

Our need for *attentiveness* to the Father is also described by a word used in 1 Corinthians 7:35, "This I say for your own benefit; not to put a restraint upon you, but to promote what is seemly, and to secure *undistracted devotion* to the Lord" (italics mine). "Undistracted devotion" is translated from the Greek word *euprosedros*, which literally means "sitting well towards."[7] *Prosedreuo* by itself means "to sit near."[8] The prefix *eu-* means "well" and strengthens the emphasis from sitting near to sitting very near or "well towards."

You've probably observed individuals so engrossed in what another is saying that they sit very near and also lean toward the person, hanging on every word. That is *euprosedros*. It's probably what Mary was doing at the feet of Jesus in Luke 10:39. No doubt this is what the two unnamed disciples were doing as they listened to the resurrected Christ open the Scriptures concerning Himself to them (see Luke 24:13-35). "Were not our hearts burning within us while He was speaking to us?" was their testimony (v. 32).

In his sermon "The Disciple's Prayer," Haddon Robinson recalls:

When our children were small, we played a game. I'd take some coins in my fist. They'd sit on my lap and work to get my fingers open. According to the international rules of finger opening, once the finger was open, it couldn't be closed again. They would work at it, until they got the pennies in my hand. They would jump down and run away, filled with glee and delight. Just kids. Just a game.

Sometimes when we come to God, we come for the pennies in his hand. "Lord, I need a passing grade. Help me to study"; "Lord, I need a job"; "Lord, my mother is ill." We reach for the pennies.[9]

When God grants the request, we walk away. More important than the pennies in God's hand is God Himself.

Prayer Is a Two-Way Conversation

I used to play a similar game with my grandpa, Bill Henkel. When we visited him as young children, he would often hide a quarter or 50-cent piece in his hand. (For you youngsters, yes, they used to have half-dollars.) After teasing us for awhile, he would give us the coin, which we knew all along would be ours. Off we would dash to the ice cream store or candy shop. (And yes, back then you could do that with a quarter!)

Years later, however, my interest in Grandpa changed. I didn't care as much about his hand as I did his face, eyes and voice. I loved to sit very close to him and ask questions about his childhood, my mother's upbringing, his conversion to Christ or just life in general. I would *euprosedros*—sit as close as possible—and listen intently.

It wasn't that Grandpa was such a great storyteller, but simply that *he* was telling the stories. I wanted to know as much as I possibly could from him and about him before he moved to heaven, which is where he now lives.

Have you graduated from the Father's hand to His heart, His face and His voice? Or do you settle for pennies?

"Great," you might say. "Inspirational. Motivating. But how does all of this relate to watchmen?" Because, the watchman aspect of intercession must entail a two-way conversation, not a one-way prayer or petition.

We can glean many excellent strategies in how to function as watchmen from Quin Sherrer and Ruthanne Garlock. The following quote is from their book *How to Pray for Your Family and Friends:*

Waiting is a very important part of prayer. Very often we must *wait* to hear God's still, small voice within our hearts, or *wait* for Him to speak to us through His Word. We would think it terribly rude if a friend came for a visit, sat down and related all his concerns, then got up and left without giving us an opportunity to speak. Sadly, many people behave that way toward God during their prayer time. Answered prayer, I've discovered, results not from some formula, but from maintaining an intimate relationship with our Lord Jesus and Father God.[10]

> As watchmen, while fellowshipping with Him, we wait on promptings, warnings and directives from the precious Holy Spirit. We pay attention, "giving ear" to Him.

The watchman anointing has everything to do with relationship, as should every area of ministry. As watchmen, while fellowshipping with Him, we wait on promptings, warnings and directives from the precious Holy Spirit. We *pay attention*, "giving ear" to Him. We listen—all ears.

In her book *Possessing the Gates of the Enemy,* Cindy Jacobs alerts watchmen intercessors to the necessity of being *attentive* to what the Lord is saying to us:

Prophetic intercessors . . . get up early every morning and "check in" with the Lord to find out what their prayer assignment is for the day. . . . Although I have things for which I pray daily, God sometimes preempts these requests for those on His heart. I have found that God's daily prayer alerts may or may not be the same as those on my prayer list. Being an intercessor [watchman] requires quite a bit of discipline in the emotional realm because often I would rather pray my own concerns than the ones that God will give me. This is when I "seek first the Kingdom of God" instead of my personal burdens.

Cindy goes on to share several ways the Lord alerts her to pray for a specific person:

- She sees someone who reminds her of another individual and realizes she is to pray for that person.
- She sees the name of someone, or a similar name, and then seeks the Lord's direction as to how to pray for that person.
- Her thoughts turn to a person she has not seen for years and knows they need prayer.

Cindy is convinced that God alerts many people to pray in this manner, but they simply do not recognize the signals.[11]

As we listen and *pay attention,* He will alert us to a person or situation that needs to be covered in prayer. We respond by praying, and He responds by answering the prayer. That is divine/human partnership.

- We speak. He listens.
- He speaks. We listen.
- We pray. He answers.

This is God and family synergistically working together for good in the earth. Second Corinthians 6:1 says, "And *working together* with Him" (italics mine). Working together is the word *sunergeo*, from which we get the English word "synergism" or "synergy." Synergism is "the combined action of two or more which have a greater total effect than the sum of their individual effects."[12] I've been told that a rope made of three strands woven together is 100 times stronger than one strand. That's synergism.

Can you imagine God saying there is a synergistic effect when we work together with Him? All of the multiplication of power must come from His strand! Rusty Stevens, a Navigators director in Virginia Beach, Virginia, tells this story:

> As I feverishly pushed the lawn mower around our yard, I wondered if I'd finish before dinner. Mikey, our six-year-old, walked up and, without even asking, stepped in front of me and placed his hands on the mower handle. Knowing that he wanted to help me, I quit pushing.
>
> The mower quickly slowed to a stop. Chuckling inwardly at his struggles, I resisted the urge to say, "Get out of here, kid. You're in my way," and said instead, "Here, Son. I'll help you." As I resumed pushing, I bowed my back and leaned forward, and walked spread-legged to avoid colliding with Mikey. The grass cutting continued, but more slowly, and less efficiently than before, because Mikey was "helping" me.
>
> Suddenly, tears came to my eyes as it hit me: *This is the way my heavenly Father allows me to "help" him build his kingdom!* I pictured my heavenly Father at work seeking, saving and transforming the lost, and there I was, with my weak hands "helping." He chooses to stoop gracefully to allow me to co-labor with Him.[13]

Grab a handle and push! Don't disappoint Dad. He desperately wants to partner with us. Where do you think our parental instincts and love for our kids come from? They originate from the heavenly Father in whose image we're made.

In the book *Intercessory Prayer*, I write a great deal about intercession being a partnering with God. As a form of intercession, the watchman anointing certainly is this as well. It is all about the divine-human partnership in which God provides the wisdom, direction and power, and we supply the body and voice. His is the kingdom, power and glory. Ours is the asking. We can't do it without Him. He won't do it without us.

It all starts with relationship—actively listening to Him and believing He is actively listening to us. Don't allow your prayers to be a one-way conversation. If they are, you will never be an effective watchman intercessor.

Listen slowly. He is.

Notes

1. Spiros Zodhiates, *Hebrew-Greek Key Study Bible—New American Standard*, rev. ed. (Chattanooga, TN: AMG Publishers, 1990), p. 1773
2. Edward K. Rowell, *Fresh Illustrations for Preaching and Teaching* (Grand Rapids, MI: Baker Book House, 1997), p. 134
3. Zodhiates, *Hebrew-Greek Key Study Bible*, p. 1787
4. Craig Brian Larson, *Illustrations for Preaching and Teaching* (Grand Rapids, MI: Baker Book House, 1993), p. 102.
5. Ibid., p. 240.
6. Elizabeth Alves, *Becoming a Prayer Warrior* (Ventura, CA: Renew Books, 1998), p. 70.
7. James Strong, *The New Strong's Exhaustive Concordance of the Bible* (Nashville, TN: Thomas Nelson Publishers, 1990), ref. no. 2145.
8. Ibid., ref. no. 4332.
9. Craig Brian Larson, *Contemporary Illustrations for Preachers, Teachers and Writers* (Grand Rapids, MI: Baker Book House, 1996), p. 187.

10. Quin Sherrer and Ruthanne Garlock, *How to Pray for Your Family and Friends* (Ann Arbor, MI: Servant Publications, 1990), p. 24.
11. Cindy Jacobs, *Possessing the Gates of the Enemy* (Tarrytown, NY: Chosen Books, 1991), p. 75.
12. *New Webster's Dictionary and Thesaurus of the English Language*, s.v. "synergism."
13. Larson, *Illustrations for Preaching and Teaching*, p. 153.

WATCHMEN ARE GARDENERS

—————————— Chapter Four ——————————

THE WEE WATCHMAN IN MY CAR

"I'm gonna blow your doors off!"

My frustration could no longer be contained on this particular morning's commute to teach at Christ For The Nations Institute in Dallas, Texas. I was running late that day, and as was often the case, my two-year-old daughter, Sarah, was with me so she could attend the children's classes.

When we pulled out of our subdivision, we ended up behind an elderly man driving an old pickup truck at about 20 miles per hour. After following him for about five minutes on a country road, we finally turned onto a four-lane highway. By this time I had totally lost my patience, and as I zoomed by his vehicle I mumbled, "Man, I'm gonna blow your doors off!"

My little girl was quiet for the next two or three miles, which I thought was rather unusual. Then, with great concern in her voice, she asked, "Daddy, why are you going to blow that man's doors off?" While watching Sesame Street, she had recently heard the story of the three little pigs and the big bad wolf who blew their houses down. Now she was picturing me literally blowing the doors off this man's truck! She had obviously been thinking about this since hearing my exclamation and was rather alarmed and puzzled.

Try explaining to a two-year-old why passing a car is described by some as "blowing their doors off." Then, of course, she needed to know that I really didn't dislike this elderly gentleman, just his driving.

About another mile down the road, I passed another car and said, "Would you get out of my way?!"

"Daddy, who are you talking to?"

"The man in the car we just went around."

"Can he hear you?" she asked very sincerely.

"No, of course not," I replied.

"Then why are you talking to him?" was her next logical question.

I thought about explaining to her that it's a very sensible thing to do because it relieves stress and causes one's driving experience to be much more satisfying and peaceful, but I didn't think a two-year-old would understand such profound logic.

After this enlightening experience, I realized I would need to be more careful about what I said. My children were listening to me!

WHAT WATCHMEN DO BEST

In the previous chapter we discussed the need for watchmen to listen to the Lord. In this chapter we are going to look at several other uses of the Hebrew and Greek words for "watchman" to help paint a clearer picture of what they do. We will discuss these individually in great detail, but first notice how the definitions—those we've already reviewed and those we will cover in this chapter—are related and even have a certain progression:

- pay attention, listen (discussed in the last chapter);
- beware, be aware, don't be unaware;
- be on the alert, stay awake, remain sober; and
- observe, be observant, be an observer; see or behold.

Let's explore these concepts one at a time, studying the various strategies they communicate.

Beware! Be Aware!

Watchmen must *beware . . . be aware*. If we are not aware, we are obviously *unaware*, or ignorant, as we discussed in chapter 1; and this can give our adversary a distinct advantage.

"Wary" is also a word related to "beware." We must be wary regarding our enemy. Webster defines wary as "on one's guard, on the lookout for danger or trickery."[1] We are not to fear our enemy, Satan, but we are to be aware of him and his subtleties.

Theologians have what is known as the law of first mention. This refers to the general rule that the first time a major subject is mentioned in the Bible, significant facts are given concerning it that will remain consistent and relevant throughout the Scriptures.

For example, the first mention of the serpent—Satan—is in Genesis 3:1: "Now the serpent was more *crafty* than any beast of the field which the LORD God had made. And he said to the woman, 'Indeed, has God said, "You shall not eat from any tree of the garden"?' " (italics mine). It is easy to see this law at work here, as the verse speaks of Satan's subtlety or craftiness. God is informing us of one of the most important things we must remember about Satan: He is far more dangerous to us as the crafty serpent than as a roaring lion.[2]

"Crafty" is the Hebrew word *aruwm*, taken from *aram*, which means "to be bare or smooth."[3] We use the same concept in our English language. Someone who is crafty or wily is often referred to as slick or as a smooth operator. Such is the case with Satan. He is very cunning, and we must be wary of his attacks and deceptions. He is always seeking to steal, kill, destroy (see John 10:10) and grab the bigger portions—and he does it with great skill.

Adam wasn't wary enough of the serpent in the garden. He heard and saw him but wasn't aware of his plans. He wasn't paying attention. Therefore, he allowed Satan to invade and violate his garden.

The devil is after our "gardens," too—our families, homes, marriages, churches, cities, etc. Our responsibility as watchmen is to keep the devil out, and this is best illustrated in Edward K. Rowell's book *Fresh Illustrations for Preaching and Teaching*.

In *First Things First*, A. Roger Merrill tells of a business consultant who decided to landscape his grounds. He hired a woman with a doctorate in horticulture who was extremely knowledgeable. Because the business consultant was very busy and traveled a lot, he kept emphasizing to her the need to create his garden in a way that would require little or no maintenance on his part. He insisted on automatic sprinklers and other labor-saving devices. Finally she stopped and said, "There's one thing you need to deal with before we go any further. If there's no gardener, there's no garden!"[4]

Watchmen are gardeners. When there's no gardener, there's no garden! Let's determine to be gardeners and keep our gardens.

This same word "crafty" is used in Joshua 9:4, describing a plan the Gibeonites used to deceive Israel: "They also acted *craftily* and set out as envoys, and took worn-out sacks on their donkeys, and wineskins, worn-out and torn and mended" (italics mine). The *King James Version* says they acted "wilily." The *KJV* also says in Ephesians 6:11: "Put on the whole armour of God, that ye may be able to stand against the *wiles* of the devil" (italics mine).

Remember Wile E. Coyote on the old cartoon show *The Road Runner?* In his devious cunning, he continually endeavored to think of new ways to capture Road Runner. Road Runner always seemed to escape, however, and Wile E. Coyote's evil plans most often boomeranged.

God has similar plans for Wily Serpent. His desire is always for us to escape and for Satan's schemes to backfire on him. Picture this same relationship between Israel and the Wily Gibeonites.

The Wily Gibeonites
The Gibeonites were one of the Canaanite tribes that Joshua and Israel were supposed to destroy. They deceived the Israelites, however, into believing they had come from a far country in order to enter a covenant with them. Joshua and the people neglected to pray about this—always a part of Satan's subtlety—

and were therefore deceived into entering a binding, covenantal agreement with them. The serpent's entry into their garden was progressing wonderfully . . . the watchmen were asleep.

The Israelites were not without warning. In Exodus 34:12, Israel was told *"Watch* yourself that you make no covenant with the inhabitants of the land into which you are going [or it will] become a snare in your midst" (italics mine). The Israelites failed in their responsibility to watch, and just as the verse warned, the snare was laid.

We can conclude from the Israelites' suspicion of the Gibeonites that God was obviously trying to alert Israel. Joshua 9:7 says, "The men of Israel said to the Hivites (Gibeonites), 'Perhaps you are living within our land; how then shall we make a covenant with you?'" Rather than heeding this caution, however, they acted on what they saw. The Israelites weren't *wary* . . . weren't *paying attention* . . . weren't *watching.* We must remember things are not always as they appear.

There is a memorable story that teaches a humorous lesson about how we perceive events:

A traveler, between flights at an airport, went to a lounge and bought a small package of cookies. Then she sat down and began reading a newspaper. Gradually, she became aware of a rustling noise. From behind her paper, she was flabbergasted to see a neatly dressed man helping himself to her cookies. Not wanting to make a scene, she leaned over and took a cookie herself.

A minute or two passed, and then came more rustling. He was helping himself to another cookie! By this time, they had come to the end of the package, but she was so angry she didn't dare allow herself to say anything. Then, as if to add insult to injury, the man broke the remaining cookie in two, pushed half across to her, and ate the other half and left.

Still fuming some time later when her flight was announced, the woman opened her handbag to get her ticket. To her shock and embarrassment, there she found her pack of unopened cookies![5]

How amazing it is to discover how wrong our assumptions can be!

Though Israel "ate the wrong cookies" and was subsequently taken advantage of, there is a positive ending to this story. Upon seeking God's solution to this problem—better late than never—Joshua received instruction that painted an amazing picture of Christ's victory over the serpent at Calvary and demonstrated His ability to reverse our failures.

The craftiness of the Gibeonites was used to typify Satan's craftiness. Joshua was told to make these Gibeonites "hewers of wood and drawers of water for the congregation *and for the altar of the LORD*" (Josh. 9:27, italics mine). The altar of the Lord, where the blood of atonement was shed, symbolized the Cross. Just as the *crafty* Gibeonites were used to prepare the sacrifices, God used Satan, *the crafty one*, to make preparations for the ultimate sacrifice—Christ's crucifixion.

The outcome of this story is an incredible assurance that God can reverse the subtleties of our adversary, the devil, and use them to bring about good. Through God's amazing wisdom, which always supersedes Satan's subtlety, our mistakes can actually become the

> A balancing word of caution: Some individuals become overly suspicious of people, and others become overly demon or devil conscious. Remember, we are to be watchmen, not watchdogs.

instruments of His redemptive purposes. This, of course, can only happen if we, like Joshua, cooperate with Him.

Have you been deceived by Satan? Have you fallen prey to his subtleties? Is the serpent in your garden? The Cross is God's ultimate proof that He can turn the circumstances around and even bring good through them.

Wily False Brethren Today

God helps watchmen by pointing out what needs to be seen and heard to aid the growth and health of a church. An excellent example of the importance of focusing on the right thing at the right time is seen in this baseball story:

> One of the classic baseball television shots comes from the 1975 World Series, in which NBC captured Carlton Fisk, jumping up and down, waving his arms, trying to coax his hit to stay fair. It did—for a home run.
>
> That colorful close-up would have been missed had the cameraman followed the ball with his camera, as was his responsibility. But the cameraman inside the Fenway Park scoreboard had one eye on a rat that was circling him. So instead of focusing the camera on the ball, he left it on Fisk.[6]

Rats and serpents, they seem somehow to go together, don't they? If you smell a rat in your situation, don't panic. God has plenty of rat traps. Through the watchman anointing you can discern the enemy's trap and set one of your own.

The New Testament has its own brand of Gibeonites of which we are to be wary. Galatians 2:4 speaks of "false brethren who had sneaked in" and Jude 4 says "certain persons have crept in unnoticed." There are people who come into churches or ministries with impure motives. If not discovered soon enough, they can do great damage. The anointing of the watchman will detect them, and they can either be exposed or neutralized in prayer so that they are unable to create problems.

A balancing word of caution should be given, however, concerning this wariness we must have. We are to be watchmen, not watchdogs. Some individuals become so suspicious of others they act more like guard dogs, not trusting anyone, than watchmen who guard only against evil.

Others are led into a deception of preoccupation when they become overly demon or devil conscious. This, too, is a part of Satan's craftiness. We must be aware and wary of him, but not so preoccupied with him that we conjure up demonic attacks and plans.

The two Greek words for "watching" in prayer mean to be on the alert, stay awake and remain sober. How descriptive! In order to pay attention, listen and beware, watchmen must stay awake and sober. Alertness is imperative. The failure of the United States at Pearl Harbor is a tragic picture of failed watchmen.

United States officials and commanders failed to pay attention in the critical weeks, days and hours prior to 7:55 A.M., December 7, 1941. If those in strategic leadership had realized the necessity to listen and beware, the results of the attack on Pearl Harbor could have been drastically different.

In meetings with both the Secretary of the Navy and the President, Admiral Richardson of the Pacific Fleet alerted them to the danger of the United States fleet remaining at Pearl Harbor. He was wary that the Japanese would realize the United States military's vulnerability and would act quickly to take advantage of the situation. His warnings, however, were ignored and he was dismissed shortly thereafter.

The commanders at Pearl Harbor, Admiral Kimmel and Lieutenant General Short, were alerted to the impending danger of war on October 16, November 24 and November 27. Not believing an attack was possible, they only took precautions against Japanese sabotage. In fact, instead of strategically moving to the logical point of attack in the northwest, the entire fleet was moored in the harbor. Some personnel were even allowed to go on shore leave. Would it have made a difference had they stayed awake and remained sober at their posts?

Four hours before the attack, a United States destroyer in the Pacific sighted a Japanese submarine. Evidently not being alert to the imminent danger, no one on the destroyer reported the attack. Also, an army private (practicing on the radar set after its normal closing time) notified his superior officer of an approaching large squadron of planes. The lieutenant, however, neglected to listen and beware, but instead passed it off as being the group of B-17s that was expected from the United States.

The enemy gained the greater portion in this attack. More than 2,300 American servicemen were killed and over 1,100 were wounded; two battleships were destroyed and six others were heavily damaged; several lesser vessels were put out of action and more than 150 United States planes were wrecked. The Japanese lost less than 100 men and sacrificed only 29 planes and five midget submarines. Their task force escaped without being attacked.

The lack of alertness and false estimation of the enemy's capabilities and intentions were primary reasons this attack resulted in such devastation. Military and civilian officials in Washington, as well as the commanders at Pearl Harbor, had failed to observe and pay attention to the many warnings of impending attack. Their neglect to listen and to beware of the approaching danger allowed the enemy's plans to be successful.[7]

Frequently, we believers ignore warnings from Scripture and the Holy Spirit. The cost is often great.

Sentry Duty

The three Hebrew words for "watchman" are also translated "observe," "see" and "behold." Jesus told His disciples to "keep *watching* and praying" (Matt. 26:41, italics mine). Colossians 4:2 (*KJV*, italics mine) says to "Continue in prayer, and *watch* in the same with thanksgiving." If we do *watch* and pray, the Holy Spirit will cause us to *see* or *observe* things that need prayer. Just recently an intercessor approached me with great concern about an aspect of our fellowship. She *pays attention—observes, watching* in prayer. And she *saw* something that needed to be prayed through immediately. I agreed. The following day we prayed with other intercessors in the church about the situation. Because she was paying attention, Satan didn't get the bigger portion. (We prayed and God intervened.)

Proverbs 29:18 *(KJV)* is a very familiar verse that describes our need as watchmen to see: "Where there is no vision, the people perish: but he that keepeth the law, happy is he." Most of our interpretations of this verse are pretty shallow.

The word "vision" does not refer only to plans or dreams concerning the future. It is translated from the Hebrew word *chazown*, which means "a mental sight, a dream, a vision, a revelation, an oracle, a prophecy." *Chazown* comes from *chazah* meaning "to see."[8] In this verse it refers to any form of communication from God to us. A good translation would be, "Where there is no communication from God, the people perish."

The Hebrew word *para*, translated "perish," is also revelatory. It means, among other things, "to make bare or naked." Moses came off the mountain and found the Israelites *para*, or "naked" (see Exod. 32:25, *KJV*), worshiping the golden calf. They were "uncovered."[9]

We often speak of "prayer coverings," or "covering" a person, event or organization in prayer. To be without this covering can create a vulnerability—people are exposed to attacks of the enemy. In order to provide this covering with the utmost effectiveness, we must have warnings and promptings *(chazown)* from the Holy Spirit. In other words, "without communication from the Holy Spirit, the people are uncovered."

On the other hand, if we are walking in the anointing of the watchman, if we are paying attention, the Holy Spirit will make us aware of Satan's schemes and attacks. We will see them and can take action.

I recall ministering in Oregon a couple years ago. My first night of speaking, I became very disoriented, confused and slightly dizzy. I wondered at first if it was a physical illness and then I began to think it was simply fatigue. I pushed through it, relying more heavily on my notes, and made it through the message.

After the service, I began to sense the Holy Spirit, alerting me that it was witchcraft. The pastor of the church strongly agreed. Upon calling home to alert my intercessors, it was a great comfort to hear they had already discerned the attack and were covering me in prayer. Some had actually sensed it and prayed *while it was happening*. They smelled a rat! It never affected me again during the conference.

That is the watchman anointing!

Pay attention, intercessors. Watch! Listen! The crafty one is always seeking to destroy lives and hinder the work of God. He is no match, however, for the Holy Spirit who is waiting to partner with you, enabling you to smell the rat and keep your garden.

Notes

1. *New Webster's Dictionary and Thesaurus of the English Language*, s.v. "wary."
2. Dutch Sheets, *Intercessory Prayer* (Ventura, CA: Regal Books, 1996), p. 244.
3. Spiros Zodhiates, *Hebrew-Greek Key Study Bible—New American Standard*, rev. ed. (Chattanooga, TN: AMG Publishers, 1990), p. 1763.
4. Edward K. Rowell, *Fresh Illustrations for Preaching and Teaching* (Grand Rapids, MI: Baker Book House, 1997), p. 146.
5. Craig Brian Larson, *Illustrations for Preaching and Teaching* (Grand Rapids, MI: Baker Book House, 1993), p. 9.
6. Ibid., p. 189.
7. "Pearl Harbor Attack" *Encyclopedia Britannica*, 1972, vol. 17, pp. 507, 508; *The American Nation* (New York: HarperCollins Publishers, 1991), pp. 797, 798; Michael Portillo, "The Attack on Pearl Harbor," *Remembering Pearl Harbor*, April 10, 1997. http://brill.acomp.usf.edu/~mportill/assign/html (accessed April 2000).
8. Zodhiates, *Hebrew-Greek Key Study Bible*, p. 1724.
9. James Strong, *The New Strong's Exhaustive Concordance of the Bible* (Nashville, TN: Thomas Nelson Publishers, 1990), ref. no. 6544.

COVER ME! I'M GOING IN!

Chapter Five

MY "LITTLE JOE" DREAM

I must have watched too many Westerns as a child. I was having a very detailed dream, one so realistic my body and mouth were into it. My vigorous kicking and unintelligible mumblings awakened my wife, Ceci, who then awakened me.

"Are you okay? Are you dreaming?" she asked.

"Little Joe," I mumbled, still half asleep.

"What? Did you say 'Little Joe'?"

"Yeah. Little Joe Cartwright." For those of you deprived of the experience, or too young to have been around, Little Joe (played by the late Michael Landon) was one of the characters on the hit Western television series *Bonanza*.

"I dreamed I was Little Joe," I repeated. "And I was fighting a big dude in a boxing match. I was terrified of him and my strategy was to keep moving so fast he couldn't hit me." Thus the kicking.

Ceci, insensitive as she was, thought it was hilarious. That's because she wasn't in the boxing ring with a man whose main goal was to beat her senseless. She still brings it up once in a while, especially when I'm having a graphic dream. "Who are you this time," she chuckles, "Muhammad Ali?"

An often used expression in westerns was "cover me." This, of course, was said by those who were running into the open during gun battles. They wanted enough gunfire aimed toward the enemy to prevent the enemy from successfully firing upon them. Little Joe said it several times. As we shall soon see, we also cover each other, not with guns but with prayer.

PRAYER COVERAGE

In this chapter we will consider five more definitions of "watchman" that will enable us to provide effective prayer coverage.

Protector

Protect or *protector* are translations of the Hebrew words for "watchman." Psalm 121:5,7,8 (italics mine) tells us, "The Lord is your keeper [*shamar*]. . . . The Lord will protect [*shamar*] you from all evil; He will keep [*shamar*] your soul. The Lord will guard [*shamar*] your going out and your coming in from this time forth and forever." Four times the Holy Spirit uses this watchman word *shamar* to assure us of His protection. The English word *protect* comes from two Latin words: *pro*, meaning "before," and *tego*, meaning "to cover; to cover or shield from danger or injury."[1] One of the ways this protection comes is through the watchman anointing. Quin Sherrer and Ruthanne Garlock share the following two testimonies of prayer coverage in their book *A Woman's Guide to Spiritual Warfare:*

> Janet's six-year-old son, Kevin, came in from school one day with a defiant, sassy attitude.
>
> "What did you do in school today, son?" Janet asked, puzzled by his mood.
>
> "Played with a crystal ball the teacher brought. We asked it all kinds of questions," he answered.
>
> "Lord, what shall I do about this?" Janet, a new Christian, prayed silently. From deep within she heard, *Break the witchcraft and curses that come with it.*
>
> "Kevin, come sit on my lap for a minute," she said, still asking the Lord *how* to follow the directions she'd just received. She gave Kevin a big hug as he climbed on her lap. Surprised, she heard herself saying, "Father, in the name of Jesus I break the power of witchcraft and curses, and I take back from the enemy the ground he has stolen from my son. We give that ground back to You, Lord. Thank you for your protection and your blessing upon Kevin."
>
> After prayer, Kevin immediately changed back to her happy, sweet-natured kid. "That was my introduction to dealing with invisible evil forces," Janet said. "In a nutshell, I quickly learned about spiritual warfare, and I'm still using it for both of my children."
>
> Kevin is grown now, and drives a huge cattle transport trailer-truck across the country. One night Janet

woke up four times, and each time she "saw" a truck going off the road. The truck was the eighteen-wheeler Kevin was driving.

"I began binding the spirits of death and calamity, then I asked the Lord to send angels to keep my son's truck on the road. I did it four times that night," she remembers.

"At dawn Kevin called to say, 'Mom, I'm back in town, but I'm too tired to drive home. Four times last night my truck almost went off the road. Were you praying?' "[2]

Janet fulfilled the role of a watchman as she covered her son from the evils of witchcraft and from physical harm. She was a *protector*—a role that is possible for each of us if we allow the Holy Spirit to help us walk in this anointing.

Keeper

Keep and *keeper* are also ways the words are used. Adam, as mentioned in chapter 1, was instructed to keep *(shamar)* the garden (see Gen. 2:15). He was the watchman, assigned by God to *protect* what was given him, *keeping* it from the serpent. *Keeping* the serpent out of our gardens is the primary assignment of watchmen.

"Assignment" is a very appropriate and revealing term. God's gifts are also His assignments. He frequently spoke of "giving" Canaan to Abraham and his descendants. Psalm 115:16 states that He has "given" the earth to the sons of men. This word "give" *(nathan)* means to give a charge, assignment or possession. God was assigning stewardship of the earth to humans. He was assigning the land to Abraham and his seed. This is why Israel had to *take* what God was *giving*.

The Lord has given gifts to us as well, which like Israel's of old are also assignments: children, ministries, churches, cities, nations and many other things. Adam failed in the assignment to protect his gift. He lost his garden. Israel, too, failed in many ways and had crop failure. We must determine, with tenacious persistence, that we will not tolerate the serpent in our gardens.

Freda Lindsay, cofounder with her late husband, Gordon Lindsay, of Christ For The Nations missions organization and Christ For The Nations Institute in Dallas, Texas, has for several decades walked in the watchman anointing. Sixty years ago they were doing and teaching what is thought today by many in the Body of Christ to be new. In her book *My Diary Secrets*, Dr. Lindsay tells of her and her husband's prayer efforts to keep the serpent out of their family garden:

> I recall when Carole began drifting away from the Lord in her high school years. And when she chose a liberal, secular college that neither her father nor I approved of, she borrowed money on her own and attended. . . . My heart was broken, and I recall one Christmas when she failed to come home I was sick in my soul. How could we be spiritual leaders when our daughter was behaving as she did? Refusing to come to church. Refusing to read the Bible. Wanting no part of anything spiritual. Wanting no part of her family.
>
> I recall one Saturday night in particular I walked the floor all night long praying, not knowing where Carole had gone. I couldn't even think of sleeping. . . . Then Gordon decided to set aside a time of fasting and praying for Carole. The days stretched into weeks, and finally I became greatly concerned about him—so much so that I was afraid he would lose his health. When I said to

him that I felt he might die from too much fasting, his answer was, "Either Carole will have to die or I will. If she continues in life as she is, she will kill herself and my ministry. So I really don't have a choice."

After 30 days of fasting Gordon felt that God had answered prayer and that she would come to the Lord, though we did not see any immediate change. But each day after that I began to claim what God's Word said about Carole's soul being saved. Through a remarkable series of events the Lord did bring Carole to Himself. She received a call to Israel and has served the Lord there faithfully for many years. I have always felt that Gordon's prolonged fasting projected Carole into the ministry which the Lord finally gave her.[3]

What God asks us to do, He equips us to do. Adam could have kept the serpent out of the garden had he relied on the Lord to aid him. We, like Gordon Lindsay, must pursue with tenacity the goal of keeping and protecting that which is ours.

Guard

Guard and *bodyguard* are also usages of the watchman words. We must *guard* carefully that which is entrusted to us, whether it be human beings or spiritual treasures. We are called to *guard* and *protect* one another both spiritually and physically. We are *bodyguards*—shields—who cover one another. Paul told Timothy to "*guard* . . . the treasure which has been entrusted to you" (2 Tim. 1:14, emphasis mine), referring to spiritual gifts and callings.

In her book *Prophetic Intercession*, Barbara Wentroble shares a testimony of the vital importance of spiritually *guarding* one another:

I remember a time when my mother-in-law experienced a flow of the river of intercession during a very strategic moment. She was sitting in her living room at 9:30 A.M. Suddenly, she felt a sensation of fear and danger, accompanied by an urgency to pray for her son (my husband) Dale. At first she did not understand where this was coming from. Recognizing she had nothing to fear and was not in danger, she asked the Lord to reveal what this was. This was a wise and necessary move, because gaining understanding is an important first step in effective prayer. An inner prompting will alert you to something your mind does not quite comprehend. At these times just ask the Lord to help you know how He wants you to pray.

After asking the Lord to reveal to her how to pray, Dale's mom then felt a deep impression that it was Dale who was in danger. She prayed for several minutes and then felt the "burden" lift. Later that night she called our home to ask Dale what he had been doing at 9:30 in the morning. "Oh, that's easy," he replied. "I remember because I looked at my watch. Another man was talking to me while we were standing out in the plant at work. There had been some remodeling in the plant over the past several weeks, and we were discussing the progress. All of a sudden I felt an urgency to move from the place where we were standing. We quickly moved to another spot about 20 feet away. Just as quickly as we moved, a large steel beam fell from the ceiling and landed in the very spot where I had been standing."

A strategic moment! Often I have wondered what would have happened if Dale's mom had not sought the Lord and received her instructions for prayer. Would Dale and the other man be alive? Could they have been paralyzed or deformed from the injury? How many tragedies occur each day because we do not know how to hear the Lord speak so that we can respond in prayer?[4]

Beth Alves adds additional insight in how we can respond effectively when God alerts us to *guard* and *protect* at strategic times:

Daniel 10 records an instance when Daniel received a message from God concerning a great conflict between the angelic hosts. The Hebrew word translated "message" is sometimes translated "burden." Often when God gives you a message or a word, there is a heaviness or a burden placed upon you to pray that word into action. Sometimes the directive will be to pray the Word of God. At other times you may be led to do warfare against the enemy forces. Sometimes intercession may cause an anguish of heart, or a wrestling within your spirit.

You must be available to receive a prayer message or prayer burden from God. And when the Lord reveals His secrets to you in this way, it is a holy trust; do not take the matter lightly. If you feel the power of the Holy Spirit moving within your heart, be obedient to cry out to God on behalf of a spiritual leader, a nation or an individual as the Spirit brings names and places to your mind. Effective prayer requires availability, sensitivity and obedience.[5]

Knowing Beth as I do, I know she practices these things. Having been a watchman in the Body of Christ for many years, she speaks with great authority and wisdom on this subject. Heed her counsel. Be available, sensitive and obedient; and you will be an effective *bodyguard* in the Spirit.

Doorkeeper and Gatekeeper

Two more protective usages of the watchman words are *doorkeeper* and *gatekeeper*. As watchmen of old guarded gates and doors of cities or vineyards, we, too, guard entrances. We are responsible and able to determine who or what is allowed into homes, churches, cities and other places.

Barbara Wentroble tells of another experience when she functioned in the role of a gatekeeper at the Lord's prompting:

> Several years ago Dale and I were part of a citywide pastors' prayer meeting. After praying for about 15 minutes, my attention was drawn to another pastor in the room. I had never seen him before and didn't know anything about him. As my eyes fastened on him, the Lord began to speak to me about him. I did not expect this. I had come with my husband to pray. The group was not used to women speaking up, and I wanted to be a quiet pastor's wife. *Lord, please tell this to one of the men pastors. I want to be obedient, but I don't want to tell this pastor what You are saying.* My begging God didn't make any difference. He just kept speaking and gently nudging me to be obedient.
>
> At the end of the prayer session, time was given for sharing anything the pastors felt God was saying. One after another shared. I kept waiting. Surely, someone had heard the Lord concerning the pastor the Lord had spoken to me about. However, no one even addressed the matter. "Is there anyone else who has heard something from the Lord?" the leader asked. After much hesitation, I indicated I needed to give a "word" to the new pastor. Permission was granted, and I began.
>
> "You are in the midst of a great conflict in your church," I said. "God has granted you an incredible gift

of mercy, and the mercy is overriding the wisdom He has for you in this situation. There is a man in your church who is involved in the finances of the church, and he is causing problems." At that moment the pastor pulled a big handkerchief from his pocket, put his face in it and sobbed so loudly it was hard to hear what I was saying.

"The Lord says you need to deal with the situation," I went on, "because it is affecting your whole church. You already know what to do, but you have been hesitant because of your mercy. If you will be obedient to the Lord, healing and restoration will come to your church. The finances will change, and you will have more than enough to meet the needs."

Quickly, I sat down in my chair as the pastor continued to sob for several minutes. Months later I met the pastor while shopping in a local grocery store. "Barbara, I have to tell you what happened. When you spoke the word to me at the prayer meeting, I knew who you were talking about. God had already been dealing with me about the situation, but I did not want to confront it. I did what the Lord said, and now our church has experienced a breakthrough. There is peace for the first time, and our offerings have increased greatly." As I thanked him for sharing the story with me, I also prayed, *Lord teach me how to hear You more and more in times of intercession.*[6]

This pastor was called by God, as are all pastors, to cover and protect his fellowship. He was a watchman. Through the prophetic anointing of another watchman to listen, he was able to guard his church and be the gatekeeper he was intended to be. Pastors, we have the right and the ability to do this.

In the same way pastors guard their churches, parents are called by God to be doorkeepers or gatekeepers of their homes. As watchmen, we have responsibility and authority from the Lord to determine what enters. We do not have to allow the serpent in! If he is already there, we should run him out.

Sometimes we must be very aggressive in our dealings with the enemy. Gordon Lindsay used to say every Christian should pray at least one violent prayer every day. He was, of course, speaking of spiritual warfare. Dr. Lindsay tells of their fervent prayer for their son Dennis when he was on a path of rebellion:

Our youngest son, Dennis, began having his problems as a result of selecting companions at school whose lives were anything but exemplary. Gordon counseled with him, and when that didn't work he would discipline him. But finally the day came when he said to me, "We will have to choose another method." We gave ourselves to more fervent prayer.

While Gordon was away, I could not get Dennis to go to school. He would stay out late at night and would want to sleep all day. When his father returned home, there was a real confrontation. Dennis ran from his own bedroom into ours and locked the door. When he didn't open to his father, his dad knelt in front of the locked door and prayed for most of an hour, calling on God to stop him in his tracks at any cost. To save his soul. To rain judgment upon him if necessary, but to use love if possible.

Dennis had not even a radio in the room, so there was no way of escaping hearing his father's praying. I am sure that prayer made a lasting impression upon his life, for shortly after this Dennis decided to go to a Christian college where he found himself and where he also met his future wife.[7]

Dennis is now a respected author and teacher and is the president of Christ For The Nations. The Lindsays knew how to deal with the serpent—with faith, aggressive prayer and persistence. They understood their role as doorkeepers.

Intercessors and pastors, we are gatekeepers, not only of our homes and churches, but also of our cities. We must guard what comes into them, and God will certainly hold us responsible for stewarding our assignment. It is both sobering and encouraging for me to read Exodus 32:25 (italics mine), "Now . . . Moses saw that the people were out of control—*for Aaron had let them* get out of control to be a derision among their enemies."

The sobering reality is that God held one man, Aaron, responsible for allowing this rebellion and idolatry. On the other hand, the fact that he was held responsible is encouraging as it communicates that Aaron could have stopped this tragedy. Had he functioned in his God-given assignment as the gatekeeper, he could have kept the serpent out. God would have supported him, squelching the rebellion, just as He supported Moses a few verses later.

Preserver

Preserving or *preserver* and *maintain* are also watchmen words. Watchmen are maintenance people. They maintain things, keeping them in good operating condition.

According to the Associated Press, on December 14, 1996, a 763-foot grain freighter, the *Bright Field*, was heading down the Mississippi at New Orleans,

Louisiana, when it lost control, veered toward the shore, and crashed into a riverside shopping mall. At the time the Riverwalk Mall was crowded with some 1,000 shoppers, and 116 people were injured. The impact of the freighter demolished parts of the wharf, which is the site of two hundred shops and restaurants as well as the adjoining Hilton Hotel.

The ship had lost control at the stretch in the Mississippi that is considered the most dangerous to navigate. After investigating the accident for a year, the Coast Guard reported that the freighter had lost control because the engine had shut down. The engine had shut down because of low oil pressure. The oil pressure was low because of a clogged oil filter. And the oil filter was clogged because the ship's crew had failed to maintain the engine properly.[8]

Many spiritual ships run aground because maintenance prayer is ignored. First Kings 8:44,45 tells us, "When Thy people go out to battle against their enemy, by whatever way Thou shalt send them, and they pray to the LORD toward the city which Thou hast chosen and the house which I have built for Thy name, then hear in heaven their prayer and their supplication, and *maintain* their cause" (italics mine). Righteous causes are maintained by prayer.

Joshua's ship ran aground and Israel's cause suffered a breakdown at Ai because Joshua forgot to pray (see Josh. 7). After their previous victory at Jericho, Joshua and Israel grew overconfident. Instead of seeking the Lord, as they had before defeating Jericho, they assumed the battle with Ai would not be difficult. "Only about two or three thousand men need go up to Ai . . . for they are few" (Josh. 7:3). Had Joshua, or perhaps one of the other leaders, sought the Lord in prayer *before* the battle, God would have told them then—before the defeat—about Achan's sin of taking forbidden spoils of Jericho. Had this been the case, Israel would not have had to suffer such a humiliating defeat. Watching prayer maintains the cause!

Watchmen *preserve*, which is "to keep in the same state; keep from decay or spoilage."[9] We keep the serpent from spoiling homes, relationships, individuals and other precious things. In 1 Thessalonians 5:23 Paul prayed for the Thessalonian believers that the "God of peace Himself sanctify you entirely; and may your spirit and soul and body be *pre-served* complete, without blame at the coming of our Lord Jesus Christ" (italics mine). The prayers of watchmen *preserve* the lives of other individuals—spirit, soul and body.

> **Watchmen are maintenance people. They maintain things through prayer, keeping them in good operating condition.**

Watchmen are also to *preserve* moves of the Holy Spirit. It is a sad fact that revivals usually wane after two to three years. They could be prolonged if those involved operated more in the watchman anointing. Paul addressed the Galatians, "You foolish Galatians, who has bewitched you . . . ?" (Gal. 3:1). They had allowed false doctrine to creep into their midst, compromising the gospel. The doorkeepers—watchmen—weren't on duty. The sentries had fallen asleep on the job and spoilage occurred.

The Corinthian church had allowed division, immorality and other carnal ways to invade their midst (see 1 Cor. 1:10-12; 5:1). Perhaps the *maintenance crew* was asleep. The church at Thyatira had allowed infiltration by the spirit Jezebel (see Rev. 2:20).

There are no doubt many reasons why improper doctrines and compromise enter churches and why moves of the Holy

Spirit are hindered or stopped. One of them, however, is a lack of prayer—watching prayer. The serpent is allowed in with his poisonous venom. Spoilage occurs. Harvests are stolen.

God is awakening us, the Church, at this hour to our powerful arsenal of weapons. We are realizing that God's plan is always for His people to win and Satan to lose. The serpent's authority has been stripped from him, his headship crushed (see Gen. 3:15).

The volunteer army of Psalm 110 is being positioned. Training is intense, but the fruit is and will be worth it. Now is the time to enlist. Enter the declared war on the serpent. You are a part of the overcoming Church against which the gates of hell won't prevail.

Run the evil one out of your house!

Drive him out of your city!

Keep him out of your garden!

Take up the challenge I once saw on the T-shirt of a young Christian warrior: "Get on your knees and fight like a man!"

Notes
1. *The Consolidated Webster Encyclopedic Dictionary*, s.v. "protect."
2. Quin Sherrer and Ruthanne Garlock, *A Woman's Guide to Spiritual Warfare* (Ann Arbor, MI: Servant Publications, 1991), pp. 214, 215.
3. Mrs. Gordon Lindsay, *My Diary Secrets* (Dallas, TX: Christ For The Nations, 1976), pp. 136-138.
4. Barbara Wentroble, *Prophetic Intercession* (Ventura, CA: Renew Books, 1999), pp. 33, 34.
5. Elizabeth Alves, *Becoming a Prayer Warrior* (Ventura, CA: Renew Books, 1998), p. 57.
6. Wentroble, *Prophetic Intercession*, pp. 59, 60.
7. Lindsay, *My Diary Secrets*, pp. 142, 143.
8. Craig Brian Larson, *Choice Contemporary Stories and Illustrations for Preachers, Teachers and Writers* (Grand Rapids, MI: Baker Books, 1998), p. 65.
9. *The Consolidated Webster Encyclopedic Dictionary*, s.v. "preserve."

WATCHMAN—LAY SIEGE!

Chapter Six

WHEN JERICHO FALLS

"See, I have given Jericho into your hand, with its king and the valiant warriors. Shout! For the LORD has given you the city" (Josh. 6:2,16).

Jericho. What a great story! Also a source of tremendous encouragement, it has for centuries spawned many wonderful faith-inspiring sermons and songs. It seemed so easy: march, shout, gather the spoils.

Your Town, U.S.A.—what a different story. March, shout, no spoils . . . march, shout, no spoils . . . march, shout, no spoils.

Frustration. Disillusionment. Unbelief. Despair.

May I remind you that in both of the above verses God said

He *had* given Jericho to Israel before there was any change whatsoever. Has He done that with you? Has He given you your city,
and yet it still looks the same?

I have good news for you. When God states He has done
something, from then on, as far as He is concerned, it is a
done deal—He *has* given. This is a chapter about taking, possessing, and laying hold of. "Fight the good fight of the faith; *lay
hold of* the eternal life to which you were summoned and [for
which] you confessed the good confession [of faith] before many
witnesses" (1 Timothy 6:12, *AMP,* italics mine). I am referring
primarily to taking cities, though the watchman connection is
applicable to any place or person needing to be captured for
Christ.

Obviously, I'm not foolish enough to attempt to do in one
chapter what others have required entire books to accomplish,
i.e., fully explain key strategies of city taking. My goals are quite
simple really: first, to encourage and to spark faith in you that
our cities can be taken for Christ; second, to connect the strategies involved in city taking with the watchman anointing.

It is well worth considering that events in Scripture didn't
always happen as quickly as it appears they did. Though the
book of Joshua can be read in a couple of hours, the conquest of
Canaan under Joshua's leadership probably took about seven
years. The entire book covers a period of approximately 25 years.
And at the end of the book, all the tribes of Israel still had not
fully conquered all of their territories (see Judg. 1:27-36).

Later in Israel's history, after a grand and glorious begin-
ning, they experienced a 16-year delay in the rebuilding of the
Temple (see Ezra 3—4). Through the ministry of the prophet
Haggai, courage and faith to continue came. Delays, setbacks
and long-term campaigns are not uncommon in the kingdom of
God. Though God has facilitated an acceleration in the pace

of world evangelization, endurance and patience are still very key factors.

What am I saying? You may not be as far behind as you think! Hang in there! We play until we win. God *has* given us our cities, even though it may not yet look like it.

Is this comparison with Joshua and Israel valid? Can we really take our cities, or is that a lofty but unattainable goal? Consider these reports of city taking shared by George Otis, Jr., in his book *Informed Intercession*.

Cali, Columbia

The Cali drug cartel was considered the largest, richest and most well-organized criminal organization in history, exporting 500 million dollars worth of cocaine a month. The cartel owned as many as 12,000 properties in the city. Drug money controlled everything, including the banks, politicians and law enforcement. Crime and murder were rampant with as many as 15 people a day killed by thugs. In the spiritual arena, the church was anemic and divided.

Then God initiated a work of prayer and unity. In May 1995, over 25,000 people filled the civic auditorium and prayed all night for breakthrough in their city. Within 48 hours, Cali experienced its first 24-hour period with no homicides in as long as anyone could remember. The police force was purged of 900 cartel-linked officers. The Colombian government began to crack down on the drug lords and, with a force of 6,500 commandos, captured most of the leaders.

Through unity and much prayer, the believers in Cali finally experienced their breakthrough. They still hold all-night prayer rallies every 90 days with thousands of people in attendance. Great openness to the gospel exists at every level of society. Across the board, church growth has exploded due to new

converts; one church has grown to 35,000 members. Denomina-
tional affiliation and location have little to do with it. This
marvelous revival has now gone on for 36 consecutive months.

Almolonga, Guatemala

In the 1970s Almolonga was idolatrous and economically
depressed. Alcoholism was rampant; poverty and violence the
norm. Families suffered terribly due to the depravity that ruled.
The gospel did not prosper; persecution of Christian leaders was
common.

In 1974, a series of five-hour prayer vigils began, and shortly
thereafter God began to move. Deliverance and healings began
to break forth, even resurrections from the dead. Conversions
began to take place at such a rate that 90 percent of the 19,000
people in Almolonga are now evangelical Christians.

The revival has impacted every area of life: families, businesses, even the produce of the land. Now nicknamed "America's
Vegetable Garden," the fields produce three harvests per year,
with five pound beets, carrots bigger than a man's arm and cab-
bages the size of basketballs.

Crime disappeared so much that, in 1994, the last of the
four jails closed. The revival continues to this day.

Hemet, California

Once called a pastor's graveyard, Hemet was filled with occult
activity and had in fact become, as Pastor Bob Beckett described
it, "a cult haven." The Moonies, Mormons, Sheep People (a drug-
dealing cult that professed Christianity), the Church of
Scientology and the Maharishi Yogi all had made Hemet a headquarters of sorts.

Gangs had plagued the city for a century, with some gangs boasting third generation members. Drugs were rampant, and Hemet Valley became the methamphetamine capital of the West Coast. Some law enforcement officials were so corrupt they transported dope in their police cruisers.

All that has now changed. Cult membership has all but disappeared, with most of the groups gone altogether. The drug trade has dropped nearly 75 percent and corruption in law enforcement is gone. Gang involvement has seriously declined—one entire gang came to Christ. Church attendance has doubled, and where there was once division and apathy, unity among churches prevails. Pulpit swapping is common and quarterly concerts of prayer and citywide prayer revivals continue to bring change.[1]

GOD IN YOUR CITY

"Great!" you may be saying. "But what do those places have to do with my city, and what do they have to do with the watchman anointing?" Everything.

First of all, the Bible states, "What God has done for one city, He'll do for another." You didn't know this was in the Bible? Sure you did. You just didn't recognize the Sheets's paraphrase. Most translations read something like, "God is no respecter of persons" (Acts 10:34, *KJV*).

Another verse says, "God wants to save people in your city just as much as those in Hemet, Cali and Almolonga." I'm sure you've caught on by now. This is an interpretation of 2 Peter 3:9 (*KJV*), "The Lord is . . . not willing that any should perish, but that all should come to repentance."

Yes, there is hope for your city and mine. There is hope for America. We are not at the mercy of sin, sinners, politicians, Satan or demons. Refuse to place control of your destiny in any of these! Choose to believe God is wiser than the devil.

If God wants to bring revival to America, and He does, then we can have revival. We, the Church, hold the keys. We are His body—His hands, feet, voice—and what He does, He'll do through us. We're Plan A and there is no Plan B.

No one said it would be easy. To the contrary, words such as "persecution," "tribulation," "fight," "warfare," "wrestle," "endurance" and others like them are all applied to us in Scripture. But so are words such as "victory," "faith," "overcomer," "conqueror," "power," "authority," "harvest" and "miracle."

> There is more to the watchman anointing than defensive or protective connotations. There is also an offensive or aggressive aspect of watching.

I want to state with boldness: If you are willing to obey God fully, walk in faith and never give up; you can have anything God wants you to have. And that absolutely includes revival in your local community.

The Offensive Power of a Watchman

What of the watchman? What does all this have to do with watching intercession? The answer to that lies in a revelation the Holy Spirit gave me in 1988. "Study the watchman concept" were the words I heard from Him.

"I already know about watchman" was my *humble* response.

"I know more than you do" was the Holy Spirit's quick and confident answer. "Study the concept of the watchman!"

He was right, as usual. It was then I discovered that there is more to the watchman anointing than defensive or protective connotations. There is also an offensive or aggressive aspect of watching. The Hebrew words are translated "to besiege,"[2] "spy"[3] and "ambush"[4] (see Judg. 1:24; 2 Sam. 11:16; Isa. 1:8; Jer. 4:17; Pss. 56:6; 71:10), because all of these things involve watching.

"I am about to release a fresh anointing to the Church," the Holy Spirit continued, "that will enable My people to take individuals, cities, regions and nations for Me. New strategies will emerge, fresh concepts of discerning Satan's strongholds will be released (i.e., *spying*) and *sieges* will be put in place that will eventually break Satan's hold over people and places.

"It will be a broad work, with strategies coming from many different sources. I will give one part of a plan to one person, another to others. This will take place simultaneously, and often one ministry or person won't even realize they are a part of a larger scheme. But I will be cutting off Satan's strength from every direction, as through the watchman anointing My people discern from Me."

This was 12 years ago, before terms such as prayer walking, prayer journeys, spiritual mapping, identificational repentance, reconciliation ceremonies, territorial spirits and others were being used. I'm sure they may have existed in some people's thinking, but most of the Body of Christ had never heard of them. And I'm relatively certain that some didn't exist at all.

Since that time literally *millions* of believers around the world have not only understood and embraced these concepts, but have *put them into practice!* The learning curve in the recent prayer movement is off the charts. In the words of Peter Wagner, certainly one of the well-known fathers of the movement, "The prayer movement around the world is out of control."

Of course, we haven't "arrived" in our understandings and

activations, but we are progressing toward the mark at an amazing pace. Fifteen years ago you would have had to look long and hard to find a ministry that existed solely for the purpose of training intercessors and establishing prayer. Now there are dozens, including several major denominations, that have entire departments committed to the facilitating of prayer. It is no wonder we are making such progress in world evangelism.

Much of the praying falls under the category of the watchman anointing. *Spying* has taken place as the enemy's strongholds and plans have been discerned. *Sieges* are under way all over the world. The watchman anointing is in place. I am so confident heaven's strategies will not fail that I have a bold prediction: *Ten years from now testimonies like those of Cali, Almolonga and Hemet will be common.*

Otis, after relating the stories of Cali, Almolonga, Hemet and several others, asks the all-important question: "Are these revivals reproducible?" His answer is encouraging:

> Bump into this same story ten or twelve times, however, and your confidence will rise. You now have an established pattern, and patterns are compelling. Laden with reproducible principles, patterns transform inspirational stories into potent models.
>
> My own investigation into the factors responsible for transformed communities has yielded several major "hits." These include, but are not limited to, the following five stimuli:
>
> - Persevering leadership (see Neh. 6:1-16)
> - Fervent, united prayer (see Jon. 3:5-10)
> - Social reconciliation (see Matt. 5:23,24; 18:15-20)
> - Public power encounters (see Acts 9:32-35)

- Diagnostic research/spiritual mapping (see Josh. 18:8-10)

Although each of these factors recurs often enough to be considered common, two of them—persevering leadership and fervent united prayer—are present in all of our transformation case studies.[5]

Strategies for a Watchman Taking a City

As we make diligent efforts to study and implement principles shared in resources such as the above-mentioned books—and doing so is absolutely essential—God will release to us this anointing of the Holy Spirit. This will enable us to transform our communities with precision and excellence. Don't try to copy these principles as formulas. The key to success is listening to the Holy Spirit give insight on how to accurately implement them in our regions.

Start immediately. It may take several years, as it did with the three cities mentioned and with Joshua and Israel, but God *has* given us our cities.

In his book *Warfare Prayer,* Dr. C. Peter Wagner shares six strategies he feels are essential to making a permanent spiritual impact on your city. Watchmen for cities should take heed to these important points:

1. Select a manageable geographical area with discernible spiritual boundaries.
2. Secure the unity of the pastors and other Christian leaders in the area and begin to pray together on a regular basis.
3. Project a clear image that the effort is not an activity simply of Pentecostals and charismatics, but of the whole Body of Christ.

4. Assure the spiritual preparation of participating leaders and other Christians through repentance, humility and holiness.
5. Research the historical background of the city in order to reveal spiritual forces shaping the city.
6. Work with intercessors especially gifted and called to strategic-level warfare, seeking God's revelation of: *(a)* the redemptive gift or gifts of the city; *(b)* Satan's strongholds in the city; *(c)* territorial spirits assigned to the city; *(d)* corporate sin past and present that needs to be dealt with; and *(e)* God's plan of attack and timing.[6]

Bob Beckett, in the book *Commitment to Conquer* (which is his personal version of the transformation of Hemet), would agree with Otis and Wagner, while also emphasizing a long-term commitment to the community to which God has called a person. His arguments and corresponding personal testimony concerning regional commitment make an overwhelming case for its importance.

I could not agree more with Bob's contention. I have personally gone through a time of recommitment to my city, Colorado Springs. In January of this year (1999), I received a significant visitation from the Lord, during which He put a new mantle and some specific assignments on me for America. There is no need for details, but it was the most significant encounter I have ever had with the Lord.

One of the results of this impartation was an overwhelming burden for this nation. It was difficult for me to mention America, Washington, DC, or even our president without weeping. The burden for America was so heavy that it became difficult to focus on my own city. This, added to the incredible pace

I have kept up the past three to four years and the resulting weariness, caused my vision and passion for Colorado Springs to diminish significantly. After some well-timed *kairos* (the Greek word for an opportune time, a distinct moment)[7] attacks of Satan, I simply had no strength of will to continue in what amounted to two full-time jobs.

By midsummer I had pretty well convinced myself that God wanted me to lay down my pastorate and call to this city in order to focus on the nation. It came as a surprise to me, when the Lord was able to finally make clear that He was not releasing me from my calling to this church and community.

I then found myself in the challenging position of needing vision and passion restored for my own city, which I'm glad to say has happened. I can assure you, however, that *as passion and love for my city waned, my anointing and ability to minister to it did as well*. If you do not have a love and commitment for your city, this is where your revival must begin.

Recognizing Weaknesses

A few of our experiences in trying to take Colorado Springs for Christ could perhaps be beneficial for some of you. We have had our share of victories and setbacks. It is not uncommon for reputations to exceed reality—sometimes negatively, other times positively. Colorado Springs would fall into the latter category.

We in our city are not where we are reputed to be in prayer, unity, salvations and city transformation. In some ways I have actually seen regression in the past seven years. The good news is that several pastors and leaders are determined to walk in unity and prayer and carry a genuine passion to see revival in our city. In spite of our weaknesses, we have great hope that this will occur.

One of the difficult paradoxes of the kingdom is to acknowledge negative realities while still walking in faith. Some in our
city have been accused of pessimism and a negative spirit when
trying to point out weaknesses. They have neither, however. It is
possible to acknowledge weaknesses while walking in genuine
faith.

The first step in fixing a problem is recognizing and understanding it. Romans 4:19, using Abraham as an example of faith,
tells us "*without becoming weak in faith* he *contemplated* his own body"
(italics mine). Though the *King James Version* says "he *considered* not
his own body" (italics mine), making it seem as though we should-
n't even acknowledge difficult circumstances, the Greek word
used *(kataneo)* doesn't corroborate this. It actually means "to con-
template or attentively consider; to observe fully."[8]

Abraham didn't grow strong in faith because he *refused* to
acknowledge the natural circumstances. He grew strong in faith
while acknowledging—even contemplating—his and Sarah's con-
ditions but respecting the promise of God so much that it carried more weight than the earthly reality.

One of the errors in some faith teaching springs from a mis-
understanding of this verse. People are taught to deny or to
ignore realities, such as sickness or financial lack. Acknowledging them is taught to be unbelief or a faith destroyer. This is
not biblical.

Applying this acknowledgment of existing realities to taking
our cities, we must honestly admit our lacks and weaknesses:
disunity, apathy, prayerlessness, past sins and others. We can
then go to God, confess our needs and find His answers. Beckett
acknowledges this is one of the things that caused change for his
congregation and city.

"For five solid years, five days a week, our church prayed
every morning for one hour. . . . We had anywhere from ten to

one hundred people at those meetings." Though he acknowledges fruit in individuals' lives, Beckett says, "The only problem
was, at the end of those five years of faithful intercession, total-
ing about 1,300 hours of corporate prayer, Hemet had not
changed one bit."[9]

He began to ask hard questions and was honest with himself
about the lack of change. When he did this, God was gracious to
give answers. He will for the rest of us, as well.

In spite of our weaknesses in Colorado Springs, there are
many reasons for encouragement. Our faith, like Abraham's of
old, is growing. So is momentum in the Spirit. Here are some
watchman activities in which we have been involved during the
last several years and which have and will continue to bear fruit.
(I am not implying that our efforts are unique, they simply are
ones I am aware of. Others, I am certain, could add to the list.)

On three different occasions, our congregation moved our
Sunday morning service to a strategic downtown park so we
could publicly worship the Lord and intercede for our city while
in this key location.

Our church and several other congregations combined our
Sunday morning services on two occasions and met together in
a nonchurch location for the purpose of breakthrough for
Colorado Springs. Others have done this as well.

For almost two years we had joint weekly Wednesday
evening services, with as many as 20 churches represented.

During the same two-year period, we led and hosted hundreds of hours of multichurch prayer meetings for our city. This
was in addition to other pastoral prayer meetings in our city—of
which there were several. Many other regular prayer meetings
also focused on interceding for this city.

In the spring of 1999, after having been warned by two
nationally known and respected prophets that the walls of our

city were down due to pride and other issues, many churches participated in 40 days of around-the-clock praise. During the same period, solemn assemblies were held for repentance of pride and other sins, along with several prayer meetings also held to intercede for the city. This resulted in tremendous breakthrough. We have credible evidence that a mass school shooting, like the one in Littleton, Colorado, was planned for Colorado Springs. Instead of following through with the act, however, the young man involved turned himself in to authorities. We believe this tragedy was prevented because of the praise, repentance and prayer—both ours and that of others.

The week after the Littleton massacre, Pastor Ted Haggard (a true watchman for Colorado Springs) and New Life Church prepared a wonderful prayer guide that lists all of our city's high schools and their superintendents. This booklet was distributed in churches throughout the city and enabled believers in Colorado Springs to pray with what Otis calls "informed intercession."[10] We believe this, too, helped ward off violence in our city.

Ted Haggard, New Life Church and the World Prayer Center are also in the process of establishing a citywide House of Prayer, seven days a week, 24 hours a day. We believe this will also help bring breakthrough in our city.

Cindy Jacobs recently oversaw a very extensive spiritual mapping of our area, with individuals from several churches working together on the project.

As a result of this effort, we have begun to implement offensive prayer strategies and recently conducted a citywide prayer and praise service at a key location. Other such meetings are forthcoming, as we are determined to take back what Satan has stolen.

These and other efforts are encouraging signs that God is, indeed, giving us insight and strategy to impact our city. We will not be satisfied until we see thousands come to Christ and our city transformed. These efforts, along with those being conducted by others, are aspects of the watchman anointing. They are spirit-led assignments of discerning (spying) and laying siege to our city.

The very concept of a siege implies time and process. Delays can be expected but also overcome. Though most revivals seem sudden, they are really a culmination of much that has happened to prepare the way. Galatians 6:9 tells us, "Let us not lose heart in doing good, for in due time we will reap if we do not grow weary." "Due time" in this verse is the word *kairos*. The point is simple: our "doing good" will create an opportune season of "reaping," if we don't "grow weary" and give up.

The Divine Shift

Since the visitation from the Lord that I mentioned earlier in the chapter, I have been to the Washington, DC, area nine times to pray and to minister. Believing God gave me a strategic assignment to do this, I have added these journeys to an already crowded schedule. My purpose has been (and still is) to generate more prayer for that city and for our nation and also to impart faith for revival in the Body of Christ there. While ministering recently in DC, the Holy Spirit kept bringing to me the phrase "the divine shift."

While meditating on this phrase, the Holy Spirit began to teach me that a *kairos* season is simply a *phase* of the *process*. In other words, through the working of the Holy Spirit in and through the Church, as well as His masterful aligning even in the unsaved world, *chronos* (the general passage of time)[11] BECOMES *kairos*. They are separate but linked. They are different but parts of the same process. We cannot have one without the other, for in fact, *it is the chronos time that produces the kairos time.*

Daniel 2:20,21 *(AMP)* speaks of the divine shift: "Blessed be the name of God forever and ever! For wisdom and might are His! He changes the times and the seasons, He removes kings and sets up kings. He gives wisdom to the wise and knowledge to those who have understanding!" This changing of the times and seasons also takes place, for example, in our individual lives again and again as we move from one phase to another. The Scriptures tell us we go from

- brighter to brighter paths (see Prov. 4:18),
- faith to faith (see Rom. 1:17),
- strength to strength (see Ps. 84:7), and
- glory to glory (see 2 Cor. 3:18).

The passage in Psalm 84 that speaks of going "from strength to strength" begins by saying in verse 6, "passing through the valley of Baca [weeping] they make it a spring." Then in verse 7 is the phrase "from strength to strength." It is in the *chronos* time of weeping, where all seems difficult and fruitless, that the work is done to allow God to transform *chronos* to *kairos*.

After God made promises to Abraham concerning the nation that would come from him through Sarah, there was a 24-year *chronos* season requiring faithfulness, commitment and patience. Though not perfectly, Abraham and Sarah made it through this time until the divine shift occurred, transforming *chronos* to *kairos* in Genesis 18:10: "I will surely return to you at this time next year; and behold, Sarah your wife shall have a son."

The word "time" in this verse is the Hebrew word *eth,* which is an equivalent for the Greek word *kairos.*[12] *Chronos became kairos!*

After refusing to believe and respond to God properly, Israel was forced to wander for 40 years in the wilderness. In Joshua 1, the divine shift occurred as God changed the season to *kairos*. "Within three days," He said, "you are to cross this Jordan" (Josh. 1:11).

After his dramatic conversion in Acts 9, Saul—later named Paul—went into a lengthy season of *chronos*. It was those 12 years of faithful study, equipping and transformation on the Potter's wheel that allowed the Holy Spirit to cause the divine shift in Acts 13, changing *chronos* to *kairos*. "While they were ministering to the Lord and fasting, the Holy Spirit said, 'Set apart for Me Barnabas and Saul for the work to which I have called them'" (v. 2).

In the 1940s through the 1980s, much of Europe was under a shroud of Communist oppression and bondage. The Iron Curtain held millions of hopeless souls in captivity, while a seemingly helpless world looked on. During this *chronos* time of seeming inactivity, much was happening in the Spirit. Untold thousands of prayers went up for the liberation of this sector of the world and the fall of Communism.

In what seemed like a day, God created the divine shift. *Chronos* was transformed into *kairos*, and the Iron Curtain came down. This didn't happen in spite of the *chronos* season; it happened *because of* what was taking place in and through the *chronos* season.

Hang in there! You may be only days from your *kairos*. The divine shift may be imminent. Your faithfulness now will help create it.

Your city may seem far from revival. Don't grow weary in your doing of good. He is faithful who promised, and He *has* given you your city. The watchman anointing is in place in the Body of Christ. Walk in it!

Let the sieges continue!

The shift is coming!

Notes

1. George Otis, Jr., *Informed Intercession* (Ventura, CA: Renew Books, 1999), pp. 18-47.
2. Spiros Zodhiates, *Hebrew-Greek Key Study Bible—New American Standard,* rev. ed. (Chattanooga, TN: AMG Publishers, 1990), p. 1752.
3. James Strong, *The New Strong's Exhaustive Concordance of the Bible* (Nashville, TN: Thomas Nelson Publishers, 1990), ref. no. 6822.
4. Zodhiates, *Hebrew-Greek Key Study Bible,* p. 1787.
5. Otis, Jr., *Informed Intercession,* p. 56.
6. C. Peter Wagner, *Warfare Prayer* (Ventura, CA: Regal Books, 1992), p. 163, 167, 169, 171-173.
7. Ethelbert W. Bullinger, *A Critical Lexicon and Concordance to the English and Greek New Testament* (Grand Rapids, MI: Zondervan Publishing House, 1975), p. 804.
8. Strong, *New Strong's Exhaustive Concordance of the Bible,* ref. no. 2657.
9. Bob Beckett, *Commitment to Conquer* (Grand Rapids, MI: Chosen Books, 1997), p. 32.
10. Otis, Jr., *Informed Intercession,* n.p.
11. Bullinger, *A Critical Lexicon and Concordance to the English and Greek New Testament,* p. 804.
12. Zodhiates, *Hebrew-Greek Key Study Bible,* p. 1763.

ARMED AND LOADED WITH PRAYER

Chapter Seven

PRAYER CHANGES EVERYTHING

When George McCluskey married and started a family, he decided to invest one hour a day in prayer, because he wanted his kids to follow Christ. After a time, he expanded his prayers to include his grandchildren and great-grandchildren. Every day between 11:00 A.M. and noon, he prayed for the next three generations.

As the years went by, his two daughters committed their lives to Christ and married men who went into full-time ministry. The two couples produced four girls and one boy. Each of the girls married a minister, and the boy became a pastor.

The first two children born to this generation were both boys. Upon graduation from high school, the two cousins chose the same college and became roommates. During their sophomore year, one boy decided to go into the ministry. The other didn't. He undoubtedly felt some pressure to continue the family legacy, but he chose instead to pursue his interest in psychology.

He earned his doctorate and eventually wrote books for parents that became bestsellers. He started a radio program heard on more than a thousand stations each day. The man's name—James Dobson.[1]

Talk about the power of prayer! The next time you're blessed by *Focus on the Family* or one of Dr. Dobson's books, thank God for a generational watchman, George McCluskey.

Many kids aren't as blessed with praying fathers.

At a 1994 Promise Keepers' conference in Denton, Texas, Pastor James Ryle told his story:

When he was two years old, his father was sent to prison. When he was seven, authorities placed him in an orphanage. At 19, he had a car wreck that killed a friend. He sold drugs to raise money for his legal fee, and the law caught up to him. He was arrested, charged with a felony and sent to prison.

While in prison James accepted Christ, and after he served his time, he eventually went into the ministry. Years later he sought out his father to reconcile with him. When they got together, the conversation turned to prison life.

James's father asked, "Which prison were you in?"

James told him, and his father was taken aback. "I helped build that prison," he said. He had been a welder who went from place to place building penitentiaries.

Pastor Ryle concluded, "I was in the prison my father built."[2]

Indeed! In more ways than one.

These are amazing stories, powerfully contrasting two possibilities. We can either build prisons for our children or through prayer build fruitful lives that bless others.

ALL WE CAN DO IS PRAY

The same stories could be told by millions around the world. Change the names, a detail here and there, but the bottom lines are the same: success or failure, life or death, fruitfulness or barrenness, bondage or freedom—results that are largely determined by the influence of righteous or unrighteous parents. Never underestimate the power of a praying parent!

In this book, we have often mentioned the concept of watchmen keeping the serpent out of our gardens. In the following quote, Jamie Buckingham comments on the importance of doing this through watching prayer:

You may not think your little field is very important. But God has set you in your field as a watchman. Most of us don't realize it, but our sphere of influence is much larger than we can ever imagine—and will continue on for generations to come, be it good or evil. It's a wonderful responsibility—frightening at times—but wonderful.

Always remember, though, you're never in your watchtower alone. Jesus is ever with you and His Spirit will whisper just the things you need to say and do.[3]

And it's never too late to start!

At a family Christmas gathering, an 81-year-old grandmother was complaining that her life was useless. "But Granny," her 31-year-old grandson protested, "you can go out of this world in a blaze of glory as an intercessor!"

It got her attention. "I don't know how to intercede for others," she said to her daughter-in-law. "Would you teach me?" That night she had her first prayer lesson as they spread out a world map on the table, got out the Bible and began to pray over various countries and for missionaries they knew. They also made a list of relatives for whom she could pray.

This "useless granny" is launched on a whole new adventure that can change her perspective on life.[4]

Unforgettable Bombs

I've often heard the phrase "All we can do is pray." That misguided statement reminds me of the amazing role played by some Czechs in World War II:

In Elmer Bendiner's book, *The Fall of Fortresses*, he describes one bombing run over the German city of Kassel: "Our B-17 (*The Tondelayo*) was barraged by flack from Nazi anti-aircraft guns. That was not unusual, but on this particular occasion our gas tanks were hit. Later, as I reflected on the miracle of a twenty-millimeter shell piercing the fuel tank without touching off an explosion, our pilot, Bohn Fawkes, told me it was not quite that simple.

"On the morning following the raid, Bohn had gone down to ask our crew chief for that shell as a souvenir of unbelievable luck. The crew chief told Bohn that not just one shell but eleven had been found in the gas tanks—eleven unexploded shells where only one was sufficient to blast us out of the sky. It was as if the sea had been parted for us. Even after thirty-five years, so awesome an event leaves me shaken, especially after I heard the rest of the story from Bohn.

"He was told that the shells had been sent to the armorers to be defused. The armorers told him that Intelligence had picked them up. They could not say why at the time, but Bohn eventually sought out the answer. Apparently when the armorers opened each of those shells, they found no explosive charge. They were as clean as a whistle and just as harmless. Empty? Not all of them.

"One contained a carefully rolled piece of paper. On it was a scrawl in Czech. The Intelligence people scoured our base for a man who could read Czech. Eventually, they found one to decipher the note. It set us marveling. Translated, the note read: 'This is all we can do for you now.' "[5]

All we can do?! The pilots on that B-17 certainly didn't have a small opinion of what these Czechs had done. Nor did the wives, children or grandchildren of those soldiers. Not to mention the lives they saved in the future as they helped deliver the world from Adolf Hitler. "All we can do . . . !"

This is often what I think when I hear people bemoan their helplessness or lack of contribution as they announce, "All we can do is pray." What better activity could a person possibly do? We can impact the world, secure destinies and affect eternity through prayer.

Prayers and Prodigals

As we think about the importance of watching intercession for individuals, most of us probably think immediately of our families, as well we should. Our personal gardens, as our opening stories reveal, are where we must begin. Quin Sherrer has taught much on the subject of praying for family members. In her book *Good Night, Lord,* she relates an occasion of interceding for her son:

> I clearly remember a day when the Lord spoke to me about my teenage son, Keith, as I walked the beach. Deeply concerned about his spiritual condition, I felt he was drifting further and further from the Lord. My only recourse was prayer. I realized that as a parent, I had made so many mistakes. So I asked the Lord to forgive me.
>
> That afternoon, as I walked alone, I proclaimed aloud Scriptures tucked away in my heart. "The seed of the righteous shall be delivered," I shouted into the wind. "Because of Jesus' blood I am righteous and my children are my seed and they shall be delivered," I paraphrased. "All my children shall be taught of the Lord, and great will be their peace," I paraphrased again. (See Prov. 11:21; Isa. 54:13, *KJV*).
>
> Over and over I repeated scriptural promises God had given me for my children. I desperately needed an

answer for my son. After more than an hour of this, I reached down and picked up a small brown shell being tossed about by the waves. "Trust me to polish and perfect your son," the Lord seemed to whisper to my spirit as I turned the shell over in my hand.

I took my shell home, cleaned it and set it where I could see it whenever I cooked. "Lord, You promised," I would say some days as I cradled it in my palm. Even after Keith left for college and I saw little change, I thanked God for His word that He and He alone would perfect my son whom I loved so very much.

Our prayer battle ended one night when Keith called to ask his father and me to forgive him; we asked him to forgive us, too. He had started his pilgrimage back to the Lord. After college and a short career in graphic arts, he enrolled in Bible school.

Not long ago Keith finished seven years of service with the Youth With A Mission organization (YWAM). . . . Today he's a godly husband to a wonderful wife and the father of two young daughters. My "promise shell" still sits in my kitchen, testimony to a prayer answer God gave me so many years ago.[6]

That promise shell is also a watchman shell, for that is the watchman anointing! Quin also shares prayer steps she uses in being a watchman for her children:

- be specific;
- pray Scripture passages aloud;
- write down your prayers;
- pray in accordance with God's will;
- pray for your children's future.[7]

In another of her books, *The Spiritual Warrior's Prayer Guide*, she and Ruthanne Garlock give biblical examples of how to do this by offering the following scriptural prayers:

- that Jesus Christ be formed in our children (see Gal. 4:19);
- that our children—the seed of the righteous—will be delivered from the evil one (see Prov. 11:21, *KJV*; Matt. 6:13);
- that our children will be taught of the Lord and their peace will be great (see Isa. 54:13);
- that they will train themselves to discern good from evil and have a good conscience toward God (see Heb. 5:14; 1 Pet. 3:21);
- that God's laws will be in their minds and on their hearts (see Heb. 8:10);
- that they will choose companions who are wise—not fools, nor sexually immoral, nor drunkards, nor idolaters, nor slanderers, nor swindlers (see Prov. 13:20; 1 Cor. 5:11);
- that they will remain sexually pure and keep themselves only for their spouse, asking God for His grace to keep such a commitment (see Eph. 5:3,31-33);
- that they will honor their parents (see Eph. 6:1-3).[8]

In chapter 6 we taught that the concept of the watchman involves aggressively laying siege, not just protecting. Ruthanne Garlock shares a powerful testimony of someone who implemented this aspect of the watchman anointing for an unsaved family member:

Sue, a former student, called one day and asked

Ruthanne to pray for her unsaved father who had termi-
nal cancer. Sue and her mother had prayed for years for
him to accept Jesus. Now near death, he was very bitter,
blaming God for his illness.

"How can we lead him to Christ when he is so
angry?" Sue asked me.

"The problem is, he's believing Satan's lie that God
is his enemy," I responded. "He needs to see that God is
his only source of help. I suggest you bind the lying spirit that has deceived him. Then just shower your father
with unconditional love; don't preach to him anymore."

Sue's mother and brother picked up extension
phones, and I prayed while they agreed: "Thank you,
Father, that it is your desire to bring Sue's dad into
your kingdom. We take authority in the name of Jesus
and bind the deceiving spirits that are lying to him. We
ask the Holy Spirit to reveal the truth that you love
him. Lord, cause him to come to his senses and escape
from the trap of the devil. We ask this in Jesus' name,
Amen."

I suggested they continue this strategy. "Use the
authority Jesus gave you to forbid the enemy to speak to
your father." About six weeks later Sue called to tell me
her father had died. But just before he died, he received
Jesus as his Lord.

"One day as I walked through the living room where
he was lying on the sofa, I went over and hugged him and
said, 'I love you, Dad,'" Sue related. "Tears came to his
eyes—it was the first time I had ever seen him cry. As I
began to share with him about the Lord, I could tell the
Holy Spirit had already prepared his heart. He willingly
accepted Jesus right then!"⁹

That is the watchman anointing bearing fruit. Siege walls were built by prayer, prohibiting Satan from continuing to lie to this father. As a result, this man is in heaven today. A similar story is told of prayer for a husband, with a few other strategies also implemented:

While visiting my friend Barbara in Germany last spring, I listened fascinated one evening as her husband, Russell, an Air Force officer, explained to a group packed into their dining room about the meaning of the Passover meal we were about to eat. As a Bible study teacher, he had spent hours preparing the lesson, the food and the table.

After we'd eaten, I helped Barbara in the kitchen. "Russ is really turned on to the Lord!" I exclaimed. "I still remember the Sunday years ago when you asked me to pray for him. He was so wrapped up in his career he had no time for God, and he was so reserved—almost stiff in those days. But now, he is not only a mighty man of God, he's a terrific Bible teacher. What did you do besides pray a lot during the time he wasn't following the Lord?"

As Barbara shared, I jotted down her answers:

- I had many intercessors join me in praying for him.
- I was single-minded in my goal—determined that my words and my behavior would make him thirsty for the Lord. I asked the Lord to keep His joy bubbling out of me.
- Russ liked to show off our home and my cooking by having company over, so I often invited Christians to share meals with us. He enjoyed that—especially meeting Christian men, whom he found fun to be around.

- The children and I kept going to church.
- Russ began to go with me to a Bible study—probably out of curiosity, but also because I had such joy. Then he started going to church with the family.

Russ finally decided to make Jesus his personal Lord. He immediately had a hunger to know the Word of God, and began spending hours each week studying the Bible.[10]

These stories point out that when we lay siege through intercession, it is essential for us to allow the Holy Spirit to give us the strategy needed at each specific moment. I always try to find the principles of God's Word that apply to my situation and then ask the Holy Spirit how to apply them in that particular instance. He is always faithful in doing this because He desires to see God's will accomplished even more than I do.

The Watchman's Prayer of Protection

As we have stressed in previous chapters, protection is an important aspect of the watchman anointing. Watchmen are guards, bodyguards, doorkeepers and, generally speaking, those who protect by covering in prayer. The following story tells of a mother's prayer for her children, which also resulted in protection for others:

Irene, a young praying mother in Texas, has formed the habit of praying for the schools her children attend every morning when she drives them there. On Mondays she gives extra time and attention to praying for the schools, the teachers and the pupils.

Last year, a few weeks into the fall semester, she felt the Holy Spirit urging her to pray over the parking lot at the middle school her seventh-grader attends. She did this for three days in a row. The first two days she drove around the perimeter of the parking lot, binding the enemy from doing any evil work there, asking God to protect everyone coming and going, and praying in tongues.

On the third day Irene got out of the car and walked around the parking lot, praying and claiming the Scripture the Lord gave her: "I will give you every place where you set your foot" (Josh. 1:3).

A few weeks later, a disturbed student from an abusive home shot the assistant principal in that same parking lot. The bullet missed his spine by two inches and lodged in his stomach. After surgery he recovered with no complications and returned to his job in six weeks. The student received much-needed professional counseling.

"I'm convinced the incident would have been much worse had it not been for the prayer," Irene declared. "We just never know what lies ahead when the Holy Spirit gives specific directions for prayer. We must be obedient."[11]

I like Irene's attitude. Some people would have immediately questioned why this incident still happened when she had prayed so faithfully. She chose to believe—and I certainly agree—that her prayers allowed the Lord to change the enemy's plans and prevent greater tragedy.

In the 19th chapter of Joshua, the word *paga* (intercession) is used several times. The passage describes the dimensions or boundaries of each of the tribes of Israel. It has been translated in several ways in different Bible translations, including "reached to," "touched," "bordered," "boundary." The *Spirit-*

Filled Bible says that *paga*, when used in this context, is the extent to which a boundary reaches.[12]

Does it surprise you that the word used for intercession, *paga*, is also translated "boundary"? It really shouldn't. It only seems logical to me that perimeters of protection be linked to prayer. I want to state emphatically: We CAN build boundaries of protection around ourselves and others through intercession. What a comfort to know that this truth is inherent in the very meaning of the word. And it is certainly consistent with the watchman anointing.

> We CAN build boundaries of protection around ourselves and others through intercession.

Strategic Boundaries

This facet of intercession is not only to be something we do on a *general*, regular basis for our family and loved ones. There are also *specific* times when the Holy Spirit will alert us to particular situations that need protective prayer. These are what the Scriptures call *kairos* times. As previously mentioned, there are two Greek words for "time." One is *chronos*, which is time in general, the general "time in which anything *is* done" (italics mine).[13] The other word, *kairos*, is the strategic or "right time; the opportune point of time at which something *should* be done" (italics mine).[14]

- A window of opportunity would be *kairos* time.
- A well-timed attack in war would be *kairos* time.
- When someone is in danger or about to be attacked by Satan, that is a *kairos* time.
- What time it is would be *chronos* time.

- The Bible speaks of well-timed (*kairos*) temptations (see Luke 4:13; 8:13).
- The Scriptures also inform us of strategically-timed persecution (see Acts 12:1; 19:23).

Ephesians 6:18, the context of which is spiritual warfare, says we are to "be on the alert . . . for all the saints" and "pray at all (*kairos*) times in the Spirit." He is not telling us to pray all the time, which would be *chronos*, but to pray at all strategic times (*kairos*). In other words, we are in a war and if we are alert, He will warn us of the well-timed attacks (*kairos*) of the enemy so we can create a boundary (*paga*) of protection by praying.

Beth Alves shares the following testimony, which illustrates this:

An example from my own life involves a favorite cousin I hadn't seen in about 10 years. I crawled out of bed in the middle of the night for a glass of water when a picture of my cousin canvassed my mind. Suddenly I dropped to my knees and began to cry out, "God, don't let Mike move! Keep him still, Lord! Keep him still! Oh God, please don't let him move! Hold him, Lord! Hold him!"

Even though I was pleading on Mike's behalf with my words, I remember thinking, *This is really ridiculous. Why am I praying this?* Then the words ceased, and when they did, I could not muster another word. So I got up, drank a glass of water and started back toward the bedroom. Again I fell to the floor and began to cry out with a grave sense of urgency. "Don't let him move, God! Don't let Mike move! Stay still! Stay still!" The words came to an abrupt end. This time I thought, *Oh, no! This must be a nightmare!*

I had no feeling inside of me other than the feeling to pray. I got up and began to pace the floor, wondering what in the world that was all about. One more time I took a few steps toward the bedroom when again I dropped to the floor. Only this time I was yelling, "Get him up, Lord! Get him to run! Run, Mike! Lord, help him to run . . . run . . . run! Let him run, God! Run, run, run!" After several minutes, a calm came over me and I returned to bed for the night.

The following day, I called my aunt to see if she could help me put the pieces together about my puzzling outcries the night before. She informed me that Mike was in Vietnam. The experience still made very little sense.

Finally, a month later my aunt called to read a letter she had received. The letter told how Mike, who was a pilot, had been shot down and landed in a tree. He had been warned to get out of the area as quickly as possible, but explained that just a few hundred yards from the crash site, he fell into a bush. "Mom," he wrote, "it was like I was pinned down. I felt like somebody was sitting on me. The Vietcong came and were unknowingly standing on my pant leg while looking up at my parachute in the tree. They turned around and began to slash the bushes with their bayonets. It looked safe, so I started to get up and was about to run when once again I fell into the bush as though someone were pushing me. I laid there for a couple of minutes when suddenly I had an impulse to get up and run. I heard a helicopter so I sprinted through the wooded area, following the direction of the noise, to an open space where I was whisked off to safety. The helicopter crew said they came in response to my beeper. And yet, it had not been working when I was shot down." That, dear ones, is intercession![15]

Shirley Dobson shared the following story of praying for her daughter, Danae, which illustrates the combined watchman concepts we've been speaking of, as well as *kairos* and *paga*:

I was at home one rainy weekend and looking forward to working on several projects I had set aside for just such a time. Both Jim and Ryan [their son] were in Northern California on a hunting trip, and Danae had plans for the evening with one of her friends. She had previously asked for permission to use the family car for her outing.

Secretly happy to have some time to myself, I turned on some music and was busy at work when suddenly a heaviness descended upon me. Feelings of unexplainable anxiety and fear for Danae washed over me. I thought, *This is silly. She's out with her friend, having a good time. I'm sure she is all right.* Instead of lessening, the apprehension I felt grew more intense. Finally, I slipped into the bedroom, closed the door and got down on my knees.

"Lord," I prayed, "I don't know why I am experiencing such fear about Danae, but if she is in any danger, I ask You to send guardian angels to watch over, protect and bring her home safely." I continued praying for a time and then got up and went back to work. The burden lifted to some degree, but I still sensed an uneasiness.

Forty-five minutes later I heard a knock on the door. Opening it, I found a policeman standing on my porch. He asked me if I owned a red car and I replied in the affirmative. "I found it upside down on a mountain road, Mrs. Dobson. Who was driving? Was it your husband?" he questioned. Danae had been driving the red car. I now realized why the Lord had impressed me to pray. Later I was to realize just how powerful that time of intercession had been on her behalf.

While he [the policeman] was there, the hospital emergency room called. They wouldn't tell me details. I found Danae very shaken with her left hand badly injured, swollen and bleeding. She had used her left arm and hand to brace herself as the car rolled over, and the car had actually rolled on her hand. We were told she could have lost her hand had her palm been facing down. Fortunately, a noted hand surgeon was in the hospital that night and was able to operate immediately. Another answer to prayer.

Later, we were to learn the whole story. Even though she had been driving very slowly, the rain had washed gravel over the oil-slick road, causing her to skid as she rounded the curve. She became very scared and lost control as most young drivers would. The car landed upside down in the middle of the road. If she had gone another 30 feet, the car would have plunged off the road and down a 500-foot embankment. There was no guardrail. With much gratitude in my heart, I thought about my prayer in light of the accident and saw legions of angels lined up against the road, keeping her car from sliding over the edge. Another answer to prayer! Danae quickly recovered, regaining full use of her left hand and we gave much praise to the Lord.[16]

Boundaries of protection! *Kairos*-timed prayer! The watchman!

Boundaries of Protection over National and Spiritual Leaders

The Scriptures also teach that we are to watch over governmental and spiritual leaders. "First of all, then, I urge that entreaties and prayers, petitions and thanksgivings, be made on behalf of all men, for kings and all who are in authority, in order that we may lead a tranquil and quiet life in all godliness and dignity" (1 Tim. 2:1,2). Dr. Freda Lindsay tells a remarkable story of a watchman's intervention in the life of her late husband, Gordon:

Many years ago, Gordon left for a round-the-world trip. Before he went, Mrs. Anna Schrader had said by the Spirit that this would be a dangerous trip. The prophecy mentioned that when Gordon got to Hong Kong as he would look to his right there would be danger. After Gordon left, Mrs. Schrader called me and urged that we get several people to pray for Gordon, as Satan was going to try to take his life. We did pray, and I committed the matter to the Lord.

Gordon went to Tokyo, and after he finished his business there he planned to go to Hiroshima. But in Tokyo the man who was to take him there suddenly found it was impossible for him to go. Gordon was greatly disappointed. He then was confronted with the decision of whether to take a train by himself to Hiroshima or to go on to his next destination.

He said he struggled all evening in prayer, not knowing what to do—wanting to go to Hiroshima but yet somewhat hesitant about going alone. Finally, after several hours of indecision and vacillating back and forth, he felt a strong urge to go on to his next destination. He caught the first plane out, and when he stepped off the plane in Hong Kong, remembering what Mrs. Schrader had said, he looked to the right. All he saw was a big Canadian plane sitting there with a long line of people climbing the ramp. His Hong Kong host appeared shortly, and Gordon dismissed the matter from his mind.

The next morning when he awoke he found a newspaper that had been placed under his door. Pictured there were the ruins of the large Canadian plane which he had seen loading! It crashed and 64 people were dead! [This was the danger to the right, confirming the accuracy of the word.]

The following day he picked up another paper, and to his amazement read that the BOAC plane he was scheduled to fly on had he gone to Hiroshima had crashed, killing 124 people! It had exploded over Mt. Fuji, killing everyone on board, including 89 Americans. It was one of the world's worst commercial disasters. The papers listed that day, March 4, as the "darkest single day in commercial aviation" with both planes going down—yet our great God was able to protect Gordon![17]

Peter Wagner relates the story of a pastor who walked in the watchman ministry and the resulting fruit. As you will see from this testimony, we often aren't aware how far-reaching our prayers can be:

A young Brazilian man named Jesuel was sent out by his local church as a church-planting missionary to neighboring Peru. Soon after he arrived, he was discussing with some friends the strategy to plant their first church. During this discussion, Jesuel reported, a demon calling himself "Prince of Peru" appeared to him.

The demon said, "Go back to your own land or you will die in Peru!"

Within a week of this confrontation, Jesuel became critically ill. He sought medical care, but the doctors could give him no hope of recovery. They informed him that, although he was young, he needed to face the fact that he was on his deathbed.

As he fought for his life, a nearby pastor, who believed in two-way prayer, was suddenly impressed by God to go to the hospital and pray for a certain young man who was there. He had never heard of Jesuel, nor did he know why this Brazilian might have come to Peru. He obeyed God, though, prayed for Jesuel, and Jesuel was miraculously healed and released from the hospital.

Jesuel then went to a town in northern Peru where, after four weeks of fruitless evangelistic efforts, he discovered that the Catholic church had not been used for six months. He befriended the church's caretaker and led him to Christ. The two of them decided they would ring the church bells and call the townspeople together for a Mass. When the bell rang, people came to the church from all directions and 100 gave their lives to Christ that day.

Many more were saved and nurtured until nearby Catholic priests heard what was going on and put a stop to it. Jesuel, however, simply moved to another place and planted five more churches in Peru before returning to Brazil to be married.[18]

Jesuel saw a lot of fruit, but an unnamed watchman also has much fruit stored up in heaven. Thank God for faithful intercessors!

Peter Wagner also summarizes a suggested daily praying guide put together by Beth Alves. The guide is focused on spiritual leaders and covers various aspects of their ministry in a community:

- *Sunday:* Favor with God (spiritual revelation, anointing, holiness).
- *Monday:* Favor with others (congregations, ministry staff, unsaved).
- *Tuesday:* Increased vision (wisdom and enlightenment, motives, guidance).
- *Wednesday:* Spirit, Soul, Body (health, appearance, attitudes, spiritual and physical wholeness).
- *Thursday:* Protection (temptation, deception, enemies).
- *Friday:* Finances (priorities, blessings).
- *Saturday:* Family (general, spouse, children).[19]

As important as this is, our prayers for others shouldn't be limited to family members and authority figures. Friends, neighbors and anyone else the Holy Spirit impresses upon our hearts should be watched over. Jesus prayed for Peter that his faith not fail him during a critical time of temptation. "Simon, Simon, behold, Satan has demanded permission to sift you like wheat; but I have prayed for you, that your faith may not fail; and you, when once you have turned again, strengthen your brothers" (Luke 22:31,32).

It seems only right that, as our example, Christ would have walked in the watchman anointing. I am sure it was His intercession that kept Peter from falling away. Our intercession can do the same for our brothers and sisters in Christ.

Neighborhood Guidelines

For those who want to begin praying for your neighbors, here are some guidelines to use as you ask the Lord to show you your own neighborhood from His perspective:

- Ask God to show you what strategy He wants you to use in reaching out to your neighbors—get-acquainted meals, coffee klatschs or similar social gatherings.
- Ask God to open up opportunities for building friendships and performing services for your neighbors. Think creatively!
- Ask God to show you any areas where perhaps you need to be reconciled with one or more of your neighbors. Confess any sins the Holy Spirit reveals in this area.
- Search Scripture for a special word for each neighbor and expect God to speak to your heart specifically.
- After any neighbors commit their lives to Jesus, be willing to continue to walk with them as they are nurtured and grow in the Word and in the Body of Christ.[20]

Praying and caring for our neighborhoods cultivates peace and kindness. Writer Quin Sherrer provides enormous insight in this area:

Could our communities be truly transformed by Christ if every neighbor and neighborhood were prayed for daily? God's heart desire is for all people to be saved and for all to "live peaceful and quiet lives in all godliness and holiness" (1 Tim. 2:2, NIV).

Christians from numerous churches in our city came together this spring to pray for our neighborhoods. The goal was for each person or couple to pray blessings over five neighbors, then to be available to them when needed. We agreed to pray: Five blessings for five neighbors for five minutes a day five days a week for five weeks.

Each member of our congregation willing to participate took a sheet of paper with this suggestion on it: Who is your neighbor? Jesus described a neighbor as someone you meet along life's road who needs your help. Think of the word BLESS to remember five important ways to pray for your neighbors:

B—Body—health, protection, strength
L—Labor—work, income, security
E—Emotions—joy, peace, hope
S—Social—love, marriage, family, friends
S—Spiritual—salvation, faith, grace

Always pray with a clean heart. The prayers of the righteous are "powerful and effective" (Jas. 5:16). Pray with compassion. Be like Christ, who was moved with compassion toward the needy (Matt. 9:36). Pray with persistence (Acts 12:5; Jas. 5:17).[21]

Miracles occur in all kinds of neighborhoods. For instance, in Charlotte, North Carolina, scores of women have conducted prayer walks. Mary Lance Sisk has witnessed many miracles in the community and notes that a great portion of the results stem from small neighborhood prayer triplets (three people praying together) that are being formed as the movement grows:

"I believe the key to the healing of the United States is going to be neighborhood by neighborhood, with women doing it!" she said. "Evangelism is a lifestyle of love which results from having Jesus' heart for the lost." Mary Lance encourages women to intercede daily for their neighbors and to pray for God to raise up a prayer movement in each neighborhood. She takes literally Jesus' command to "Love your neighbor as yourself," and Peter's admonition to "proclaim the praises of Him who called you out of darkness into His marvelous light" (1 Pet. 2:9, *NKJV*).

Walking on her street, she makes it a habit to proclaim Scripture. "Lord, we invite the King of Glory to come in. Come forth and bring Your glory into this neighborhood. Release Your blessing to the families here." One of her neighborhood's most successful events is called "Meet You At The Corner." The neighbors gather on the Saturday morning before Easter for a short service declaring "He is Alive." They share refreshments and fellowship. Flyers are distributed door to door—even the children come along with their parents.

"We're able to share about the resurrected Lord in a contextual way," Mary Lance said. "It's one of the best ways in the world to meet your neighbors."[22]

Walking in the Compassion
of the Greatest Watchman

Whether praying for family members, leaders, friends or neighbors, one of the greatest keys to walking in the watchman calling is to allow oneself to walk in the compassion of the greatest Watchman. As we partake of Christ's High Priest anointing, we too will be touched with the feelings of others' infirmities.

Joseph Damien was a nineteenth-century missionary who ministered to people with leprosy on the island of

Molokai, Hawaii. Those suffering grew to love him and revered the sacrificial life he lived out before them. One morning before Damien was to lead daily worship, he was pouring some hot water into a cup when the water swirled out and fell onto his bare foot. It took him a moment to realize that he had not felt any sensation. Gripped by the sudden fear of what this could mean, he poured more hot water on the same spot. No feeling whatsoever.

Damien immediately knew what had happened. As he walked tearfully to deliver his sermon, no one at first noticed the difference in his opening line. He normally began every sermon with "My fellow believers." But this morning he began with, "My fellow lepers."[23]

My fellow watchmen, most of us will never be called to be a leper to save others. Our lives will probably not be laid down in a literal sense, but every believer is called to a life of prayer. We are also called to be our brother's *keeper*—yes, the word is "watchman." Let the love of God constrain you to pick up the serpent-killing mantle God is offering.

Use it daily!

Notes

1. Edward K. Rowell, *Fresh Illustrations for Preaching and Teaching* (Grand Rapids, MI: Baker Book House, 1997), p. 165.
2. Ibid., p. 68.
3. Jamie Buckingham, *The Nazarene* (Ann Arbor, MI: Servant Publications, 1991), p. 89.

4. Quin Sherrer and Ruthanne Garlock, *How to Pray for Your Family and Friends* (Ann Arbor, MI: Servant Publications, 1990), p. 79.

5. Craig Brian Larson, *Illustrations for Preaching and Teaching* (Grand Rapids, MI: Baker Book House, 1993), p. 219.

6. Quin Sherrer, *Good Night, Lord* (Ventura, CA: Regal Books, 2000), pp. 164, 165.

7. Quin Sherrer, *How to Pray for Your Children* (Ventura, CA: Regal Books, 1998), p. 24.

8. Quin Sherrer and Ruthanne Garlock, *The Spiritual Warrior's Prayer Guide* (Ann Arbor, MI: Servant Publications, 1992), pp. 158, 159.

9. Quin Sherrer and Ruthanne Garlock, *A Woman's Guide to Spiritual Warfare* (Ann Arbor, MI: Servant Publications, 1991), pp. 32, 33.

10. Sherrer and Garlock, *How to Pray for Your Family and Friends*, pp. 43, 44.

11. Ibid., pp. 34, 35.

12. *The Spirit-Filled Bible—KJV* (Nashville, TN: Thomas Nelson Publishers, 1991), pp. 331, 332.

13. Ethelbert W. Bullinger, *A Critical Lexicon and Concordance to the English and Greek New Testament* (Grand Rapids, MI: Zondervan Publishing House, 1975), p. 804.

14. Ibid.

15. Elizabeth Alves, *Becoming a Prayer Warrior* (Ventura, CA: Renew Books, 1998), pp. 29, 30.

16. Cindy Jacobs, *The Voice of God* (Ventura, CA: Regal Books, 1995), pp. 176-178.

17. Mrs. Gordon Lindsay, *My Diary Secrets* (Dallas, TX: Christ For The Nations, 1976), pp. 181-183.

18. C. Peter Wagner, *Praying with Power* (Ventura, CA: Regal Books, 1997), pp. 57, 58.

19. C. Peter Wagner, *Prayer Shield* (Ventura, CA: Regal Books, 1992), p. 177.

20. Sherrer and Garlock, *How to Pray for Your Family and Friends*, pp. 95, 96.

21. Sherrer, *Good Night, Lord*, pp. 83, 84.

22. Quin Sherrer and Ruthanne Garlock, *A Woman's Guide to Spirit-Filled Living* (Ann Arbor, MI: Servant Publications, 1996), pp. 227, 228.

23. Rowell, *Fresh Illustrations for Preaching and Teaching*, p. 124.

KEEPING WATCH OVER YOURSELF

Chapter Eight

MY FATHER-IN-LAW'S TEST

My father-in-law, James Merchant, is a watchman for his family. I've now assumed the primary role of watching over his daughter, Ceci, but for years he did an admirable job. Actually, her real name is Celia—that's what he calls her (pronounced by him and others in Mississippi "Say-ya").

I'll never forget my first meeting with him. Ceci and I met in Bible school, and I had already decided I wanted to marry her before her mom and dad met me. Mr. James Watchman-for-Say-ya-Merchant decided on his own unique way of checking my work ethic and submission to elders on my first visit to their farm.

After a wonderful Mississippi breakfast of bacon, eggs and the absolutely best biscuits in the world made by my mother-in-law, Melba, James said to me, "I need some help with the cows today."

"Sure," I said, looking for ways to prove I was worthy of his daughter.

We then proceeded to vaccinate and tag 40 calves. My job was to catch them, push them down the chute and hold them, while James did the smart work of tagging and vaccinating. Scared baby calves do the same thing scared puppies do—mess all over themselves. Correction, they mess all over themselves and whomever happens to be scaring, catching, pushing and holding them *from behind.*

By the time we finished, I was an amazing mixture of mud, perspiration, calf manure and urine—pretty much from head to toe. Mr. James Watchman-for-Say-ya-Merchant was as clean as a whistle and smiling from ear to ear.

On our return from the barn, Say-ya met us outside with a big smile of her own. Being as absolutely crazy about me as she was, her whole world revolved around my passing this test. Seeing her daddy's smile, she knew all was well. Still grinning herself, she began—from a distance, due to my odorous condition—hosing me off. Strangely, for the next two weeks people seemed to avoid me like the plague. I was a little rank for awhile—even the dogs didn't come near me—but I was a happy man.

Pity the poor guys who come asking Mr. Dutch Watchman-for-Sarah-and-Hannah-Sheets for my daughters' hands in marriage one day. I've had 22 years so far to reflect and to improve on this testing process.

We've spoken about watching for many things throughout this book—nations, cities, neighborhoods, harvests, individuals (daughters—get 'em, James!)—but the watching target of this chapter may surprise you: It's ourselves. While not primarily related to prayer, this certainly has to do with the watchman anointing.

GUARD YOUR HEART

"Watch over your heart with all diligence for from it flows the springs of life" (Prov. 4:23, italics mine). "Watch" is translated from *natsar,* one of our words for watchman. Yes, as important as it is to watch for others, we are also to be watchmen for our own hearts, guarding what we allow to enter. The word "heart" in this verse is the Hebrew word *leb.* Although this could mean the physical heart, it is used "figuratively for the feelings, the will and even the intellect."[1] This would include the soul—the mind, will and emotions. Again, we are told to be watchmen over them with all diligence.

Deuteronomy 4:15,23 instructs us to watch and guard against idolatry. Deuteronomy 6:12 tells us to watch ourselves, making certain blessing and prosperity don't cause us to forget the Lord. There are many areas we must watch, and as door-keepers of our own souls we determine what is allowed in, which then determines who we are in word and in deed.

Proverbs 23:7 gives tremendous insight to this, "For as he thinks within himself, so he is." "Thinks" *(shaar)* is a very interesting word. In fact, it's a watchman word. It doesn't literally mean to think; that was a derived, figurative meaning. It actually means "to split or open; to act as a gatekeeper."[2] In other words, we are who we are because of what is allowed into our minds, *causing* a particular way of thinking. The verse is actually saying, "Whatever a person lets into his soul, so he will be." Each of us is the product of what we allow to access our minds and hearts. The context of the verse, in keeping with this reasoning, tells us to be careful with whom we associate. We are, indeed, watchmen for our own souls—our minds and emotions. It is critical that we act as gatekeepers or doorkeepers of our hearts.

Further explanation of the way the mind works will help us as watchmen. We, as human beings, are not controlled by that which is true. We are controlled by *what we believe to be true,* whether it is or not. Deceptions, lies and distorted perceptions all can control us, even though untrue. This is the biblical concept of a stronghold—a prison in the mind (see 2 Cor. 10:4) built by the distortions and deceptions of the enemy.

Even latent beliefs, buried deep in our subconscious, control us whether true or not. An article in *Readers Digest* stated that "when people who fear snakes are shown a picture of a snake, sensors on their skin will detect sweat, a sign of anxiety, even though the people say they do not feel fear. The sweat shows up even when a picture is presented so rapidly that the subject has no conscious awareness of seeing it."[3]

Once a concept or philosophy has embedded itself into the deepest recesses of one's mind and memory, the belief center, the mind considers it to be truth and functions accordingly. And what is believed to be true *will* control the person, whether it is true or not. Thus Proverbs says, "So he [or she] is" (Prov. 23:7).

I once knew a lady who, for the first three years of her marriage, was unable to enter a physical union with her husband. She had been molested as a child, and though she tried to convince herself that her todays didn't need to be controlled by her yesterdays, she was unsuccessful. The stronghold in her belief center was too strong. A siege was necessary. As is often the case, her key to freedom was forgiving, which released the Holy Spirit to do the necessary work in her soul—her mind and emotions.

Comparing the human soul to the rings of a tree is helpful in understanding strongholds. The history of a tree can be read in its annual rings. If there has been drought, it will show in the rings. The same is true for plagues of insects, fires and also healthy years.

In the same way, everything we have experienced is recorded in our souls. If we could slice them open and see their "rings," we could read their histories. We might see great rejection in one year and the death of someone close, molestation or other harmful events in other years. Though some of what happens is beyond our control, these events can still lead to strongholds.

This is why Proverbs 4:23 says we must guard our souls, carefully determining what is allowed to enter. And though we cannot control everything placed there, we can be gatekeepers who strategically watch over what does and doesn't have access. If we do not, Satan will succeed in establishing strongholds.

Strongholds in the Heart and Mind

But what if strongholds already exist in a person's mind or emotions? Many people have allowed in much unbiblical information before becoming Christians. Others have allowed great amounts of perversion and unclean thinking to be engrained into their souls. Still others have experienced great trauma, rejection or other emotional wounds before coming to Christ. All of these things can be used to establish strongholds within them, causing certain patterns of acting and thinking.

A person doesn't have to be born again long before discovering that the new birth did not erase all that had been previously programmed into the mind and emotions. We can certainly guard what comes into our souls in the future, but what of the strongholds, wrong ways of thinking, fears and other destructive soul patterns already there?

We must *lay siege* to them! As mentioned previously, "watch" in Proverbs 4:23 is *natsar* (one of our watchman words) and also means "to lay siege." By the power of the Holy Spirit we can see these strongholds torn down. "The weapons we fight with . . . have divine power to demolish strongholds" (2 Cor. 10:4,5, *NIV*). The New Testament calls this renewing our minds (see Rom. 12:1,2), which is done through the Word of God. I have wonderful news for you—there is hope for a troubled, bound or wounded soul!

The Liberating Power of God's Word

How do we accomplish this renewing of the soul? First of all, we must remember that a siege implies a process over time. One of the misconceptions of trying to renew the soul is assuming it can be changed simply by a quality choice. In reality, however, a person is not able to overcome a stronghold, established mindset or habit just by choosing to be different. That is only the first step of a *process*. What must be chosen is the *process of change*. I realize you probably don't like that—I don't either. When I need fixing, I want to be fixed quickly. But if it were that simple, New Year's resolutions would work. I rest my case.

> All truth from God comes in seed form. What you do with the seed after it is planted will determine whether or not it bears fruit in you.

Several years ago the Holy Spirit spoke a phrase to my heart that tremendously helped me understand this process. I was thinking about John 8:32, "And you shall know the truth, and the truth shall make you free." Knowing this verse was speaking about the truth of His Word, I was wondering why it hadn't become reality in my life.

Most of us, if honest, would have to acknowledge that our experiences don't always line up with the Scriptures. For example, we are more than conquerors, but we are sometimes conquered by bad attitudes, sin, unbelief or other weaknesses. We're told we need never fear, but most Christians do.

Why doesn't the Word work for me? I thought while meditating about this verse in John.

Because all truth comes in seed form, He so clearly spoke to my heart. *What you do with the seed after it is planted will determine whether or not it bears fruit in you.*

Suddenly, many other passages of Scripture made sense: the parables of the sower (see Matt. 13; Mark 4; Luke 8); the renewing of the mind (see Rom. 12:1,2); abiding in the Vine by abiding in His Word (see John 15) and others. All of these involve planting seeds and working the process.

I discovered, that day and during subsequent studies, that this process of applying God's Word is both *constructive* and *destructive.* It is a healing scalpel and a destroying sword. It is a watering nutrient and a pruning knife. Through it God gives life to those who believe and releases judgment to those who don't. And most importantly, I realized its work in me was a process.

The word "transformed" in Romans 12:2 and 2 Corinthians 3:18 confirms this. It is *metamorphoo,* from which we get the English word "metamorphosis." The concept is a process of change from one form or state to another from the inside out. The Holy Spirit within wants to go to work on us, changing what is contrary to Scripture that produces unwholeness in us. His greatest surgical tool is the Word.

In 1977 I witnessed a horribly gruesome automobile accident. The violence was indescribable. Being one of the first on the scene, I watched a young man die. Through the trauma of this event, a spirit of fear tried to overpower me. Using the indelibly imprinted scene I had witnessed, with relentless tenacity, it warred against my soul.

I felt fear all the time. I felt fear of being alone, fear of the dark, fear of the unknown and fear of just about everything imaginable. I couldn't sleep at night because of the replayed horror I had witnessed and the spirit that was using it. I *knew* this was a spirit of fear, trying to use this trauma to create a stronghold. Somehow I realized if I ever yielded to the fear, it would then own me. By refusing to act on it, I didn't yield to it but always pushed through and did what I needed to do in spite of the feelings of fear.

The Holy Spirit made real to me the incredible power of His Word as a sword. He showed me that I would have to wage all-out war against this spirit and the trauma to my emotions by using "the sword of the Spirit, which is the word of God" (Eph. 6:17). I obeyed. For close to a month, nearly all the time, I meditated on and spoke Scriptures concerning freedom from fear. Every possible moment I kept God's Word on my mind and tongue—I was laying siege, releasing the anointing.

I believe it took so long because of the incredible trauma to my emotions when I witnessed the gruesome accident. But one day, as suddenly as it came, the fear and the spirit left. The Word had made me free, the seeds had born fruit, the siege was successful.

Hebrews 4:12,13 describes laying siege to the soul with the Word: "For the word of God is living and active and sharper than any two-edged sword, and piercing as far as the division of soul and spirit, of both joints and marrow, and able to judge the thoughts and intentions of the heart. And there is no creature hidden from His sight, but all things are open and laid bare to the eyes of Him with whom we have to do."

These wonderful verses give tremendous insight to the transforming ability of the Scriptures to heal that which needs healing and destroy the strongholds in the soul. The words "laid bare" in verse 13 are from the Greek word *trachelizo*, which literally means "to seize and bend back the neck, exposing the throat, as with an animal being slaughtered or sacrificed."[4] The word was also used to describe battlefield action. Need I say more?

Ugly? Yes. Graphic? Very.

But this strong and violent word is describing what His Word can do—not to us—but to the problem areas of the soul. We are meant to see the power of His Word and the intensity of our great High Priest against those things in our souls that work against our well-being and the life of His Spirit.

Though we are guilty of sin and rebellion toward God, He brings us life through His Word and His Spirit. This story of a war memorial often reminds me of how believers can be counted as dead in sin but be made alive in Christ:

> The Vietnam Veteran's Memorial is striking for its simplicity. Etched in a black granite wall are the names of 58,156 Americans who died in that war. Since its opening in 1982, the stark monument has stirred deep emotions. Some visitors walk its length slowly, reverently, and without pause. Others stop before certain names, remembering their son or sweetheart or fellow soldier, wiping away tears, tracing the names with their fingers.
>
> For three Vietnam veterans—Robert Bedker, Willard Craig, and Darrall Lausch—a visit to the memorial must be especially poignant, for they can walk up to the long ebony wall and find their own names carved in the stone. Because of data-coding errors, each of them was incorrectly listed as killed in action.

Dead, but alive—a perfect description of the Christian.[5]

God has some wonderful lists in heaven. One list contains "the certificate of debt consisting of decrees against us" (Col. 2:14). It contains all the curses resulting from sin, all of our weaknesses, bruises, wounds and fears. Your name is on one such list, followed by the phrase "crucified with Christ" (Gal. 2:20). There is another list called the Lamb's book of life (see Rev. 13:8). If you're born again, your name is there as well, followed by the phrase "nevertheless [he/she] live[s]" (Gal. 2:20, *KJV*). We are, indeed, dead but alive.

Hebrews 4:12 speaks of this life and death and is amazingly rich with promise. A short summary will bless, equip and encourage you in your work of laying siege to the soul. Here are some amplifications:

"The Word of God is *living*" (italics mine). "Living" comes from the Greek word *zao* from *zoe*, which means the life of God— "actively alive."[6] The Word of God is also *"active"* (italics mine). In Greek "active" is *energas*—"working, toiling, operative, effectual, energized."[7] An amplification of the verse to this point might be: "The Word of God is alive—actively alive—it is filled with the life of God and is full of His energy. It toils and works in us and is operative and effectual." In addition, the Word of God is *"piercing"* (italics mine). "Piercing" comes from the word *diikneomai:* from *dia*—"the channel of an act"; and from *hikanos*—"to arrive; competent, ample, attain the desired end, sufficient, adequate, enough."[8]

Let's add this to the amplification we already have: "The Word of God is alive—actively alive—it is filled with the life of God and is full of His energy. It toils and works in us and is operative and effectual. It is sharp enough and is fully competent (adequate, sufficient, ample, has enough ability) to channel itself through the various areas of the soul and spirit, reaching its desired end and attaining its desired goal. It is fully adequate! It will arrive! And it will accomplish its goal once it gets there!"

Wow! What a promise!

Moreover, in "as far as the *division* of soul and spirit" (italics mine), the word "division" comes from *merismos,* which means "a separation and distribution; to divide or disunite; to apportion."[9] The Word of God will *divide* or *separate* the soul and spirit, *distributing* to each what it needs, and the phrase "and able to *judge*" comes from *kritikos*—"to judge or critique."[10]

One more time! "The Word of God is alive—actively alive—it is filled with the life of God and is full of His energy. It toils and works in us and is operative and effectual. It is sharp enough and fully competent (adequate, sufficient, ample, has enough ability) to channel itself through the various areas of the soul and spirit, reaching its desired end and attaining its desired goal. It is fully adequate! It will arrive and will accomplish its goal once it gets there! It will divide between the soul and spirit, apportioning to each what is needed as it critiques the thoughts and intentions of the heart." Now let's add an amplification of verse 13 to the mix: "when necessary it lays the knife to the throat of anything found in the soul that is contrary to His Word."

How's that for laying siege! Yes, as watchmen, we guard the entrance to our souls. But we also deal aggressively with anything already working there that wars against the spirit. With the sword of the Spirit, we drive it out!

A soul that has been transformed—successfully laid siege to—by the Word is a weaned soul. Have you ever heard of a weaned soul? I didn't think so. The Bible speaks of one, however. The word is *gamal,* meaning "ripen, mature, wean."[11] It is sometimes translated "deal bountifully" because when a plant has bountiful provision, it *matures* and the fruit *ripens.* When a baby has bountiful provision, it *matures* and is *weaned*. Psalms 116:7, 131:1,2 and 142:7 use this word to speak of the soul.

"Return to your rest, O my soul, for the LORD has *dealt bountifully* with you" (Ps. 116:7, italics mine).

"O LORD, my heart is not proud, nor my eyes haughty; nor do I involve myself in great matters, or in things too difficult for me. Surely I have composed and quieted my soul; like a *weaned* child rests against his mother, my soul is like a *weaned* child within me" (Ps. 131:1,2, italics mine).

"Bring my soul out of prison, so that I may give thanks to Thy name; the righteous will surround me, for Thou wilt *deal bountifully* with me" (Ps. 142:7, italics mine).

God wants our souls to be well fed by His word, growing strong and maturing to the point that we think the way He thinks. He wants them weaned of pride, carnality and bondages. His desire is for us to lay siege to any strongholds of the enemy there, allowing the sword of His Word to slay all that is opposed to Him. Watchmen are warriors and sometimes the war is within themselves!

Once we have our souls weaned from that which oppresses them, they can be at rest, as stated in the above verses from Psalms 116 and 131. God wants us to have restful souls that truly walk in His peace. If there is a part of your soul that is not yet under the peaceful influence of your Shepherd, the Holy Spirit will help you lay siege to it, freeing you from that stronghold.

Take up your watchman sword and go to war. He guarantees your victory.

Notes

1. James Strong, *The New Strong's Exhaustive Concordance of the Bible* (Nashville, TN: Thomas Nelson Publishers, 1990), ref. no. 3820.

2. Ibid., ref. no. 8176.

3. Daniel Goleman, "What's Your Emotional IQ?" *Readers Digest*, January 1996, p. 50.

4. Spiros Zodhiates, *The Complete Word Study Dictionary* (Iowa Falls, IA: Word Bible Publishers, 1992), p. 1393.

5. Craig Brian Larson, *Illustrations for Preaching and Teaching* (Grand Rapids, MI: Baker Book House, 1993), p. 47.

6. Strong, *New Strong's Exhaustive Concordance of the Bible*, ref. no. 2198.

7. Ibid., ref. no. 1756.

8. Ibid., ref. no. 1338.

9. Ibid., ref. no. 3311.

10. Ibid., ref. no. 2924.

11. Ibid., ref. no. 1580.

THE WATCHMAN'S ALLY

Chapter Nine

PARTING IN OUR BEST INTERESTS

"It is better for you that I leave," is what Jesus told His followers (see John 16:7). What a seemingly ridiculous, asinine statement! After watching Him raise the dead, heal lepers, walk on water, calm raging storms with a word, deliver the insane, pay taxes with fish-mouth money—the list seems endless—can you imagine the shock of the disciples at such a statement?

Of course, He was forever shocking them with His words and actions. They must have thought with surprise and astonishment, "There He goes again!" I can almost see them waiting until He turned His head and then rolling their eyes at one another.

A short time before, He had mentioned going to prepare dwelling places for them in the presence of Father. "Of course, you know where I'm going," He stated rather matter of factly (John 14:4, Sheets's paraphrase).

"We don't have the slightest idea what you're talking about" (Sheets's paraphrase of John 14:5), Thomas finally had the brass to say. Thank God for Thomas! If he could express his frustration at some of God's words and ways, so can I. (And I do once in a while!)

Peter also spoke out his frustration at times. On a different occasion, he finally had enough of Christ's seemingly confusing words and decided Jesus just needed a good rebuke. Unlike Thomas, he *didn't* get away with it. I suppose the lesson learned is this: plead ignorance with God; disagree even, but don't rebuke Him.

Jesus' declaration in John 16:7 that His leaving would be good for them was probably different, however. It was one thing to see and hear things beyond their comprehension. But when Jesus started talking about suffering, dying or, as in this case, leaving, I imagine that started pushing a few panic buttons.

How could His leaving possibly be advantageous for them? He was God in the flesh, for heaven's sake. The answer lies in two understandings. The first has to do with Christ's choice of the word "advantage," or as the *KJV* says, "expedient." The word is *sumphero* and literally means "to bring together."[1] Since the *bringing* of right things or people *together* produces benefit, advantage or profit, the word was used for these concepts of advantage or expediency.

Christ was saying in essence, "My leaving will cause a new connection, a joining together which will be of tremendous benefit to you ... yes, of even greater benefit than My actually being here with you."

The second necessary contextual understanding is simply with whom that new connection would be. Jesus was, of course, speaking of the Holy Spirit. "I will bring you together with the Holy Spirit." "This," He was stating, "will be even more *advantageous* than having Me here with you in the flesh. The bodily limitation of My being in only one place at a time will not be so with Him. In fact, not only will He be *with* you, He'll be *in* you. *You will become His body—His hands, feet and mouth! He'll touch through you, speak through you and move through you.*"

I don't think any of us have fully grasped the ramifications of this. Our operative "mere men" (see 1 Cor. 3:3) levels of fruit and power confirm this assertion. Suffice it to say Jesus meant it when He said, "It's better for you if I leave."

Craig Larson offers this illustration:

Consider the power and greatness of the One who created the universe and inhabits every square inch.

Begin with our solar system. At the speed of light, 186,000 miles a second, sunlight takes eight minutes to reach the earth. That same light takes five more hours to reach the farthest planet in our solar system, Pluto. After leaving our solar system that same sunlight must travel for four years and four months to reach the next star in the universe. That is a distance of 40 trillion kilometers—mere shoutin' distance in the universe!

The sun resides in the Milky Way Galaxy, which is shaped like a flying saucer, flat and with a bulge in the center. Our sun is roughly three-quarters of the way to the edge of the galaxy. To get a feel for that distance, if our solar system were one inch across, the distance to the center of the Milky Way Galaxy would be 379 miles. Our galaxy contains hundreds of billions of stars.

Yet the Milky Way is but one of roughly one trillion galaxies in the universe. Says astronomer Allan Sandage, "Galaxies are to astronomy what atoms are to physics."

There are twenty galaxies in what is called our local group. The next sort of grouping in the universe is called a supercluster of galaxies. Within our supercluster, the nearest cluster of galaxies, called Virgo, is 50 million light years away. (A light year is the distance light travels in one year. To get a feel for the distance of one light year, if you drove your car at 55 miles per hour, it would take you 12.2 million years to travel one light year.)

Astronomers estimate that the distance across the universe is roughly 40 billion light years and that there are roughly 100 billion trillion stars.

And the Lord Almighty is the Creator of it all.[2]

This God dwells in you! What could we be with true revelation of this? Probably true Christians—little Christs!

Listen to two leading Christian voices describe the work of the Holy Spirit in their lives. Jack Hayford says:

- It is the Spirit who keeps the Word alive, and progressively being "incarnated" in me.
- It is the Spirit who infuses prayer and praise with passion and begets vital faith for the supernatural.
- It is the Spirit who teaches and instructs me so that the "mirror" of the Word shines Jesus in and crowds sin out.
- It is the Spirit who brings gifts and giftedness for power-ministry to my life.
- It is the Spirit who will bring love, graciousness, and a spirit of unity to my heart; so that I not only love

the lost and want to see people brought to Christ,
but I love all other Christians, and refuse to become
an instrument of injury to Christ's body—the
Church.³

Bill Bright states it this way:

- He guides us (John 16:13), empowers us (Mic. 3:8) and
  makes us holy (Rom. 15:16). He bears witness in our
  lives (Rom. 8:16), comforts us (John 14:16-26), gives us
  joy (Rom. 14:17).
- As our teacher of spiritual truths, the Holy Spirit illu-
  minates our minds with insights into the mind of
  Christ (1 Cor. 2:12,13) and reveals to us the hidden
  things of God (Isa. 40:13,14).
- As you are filled with the Holy Spirit, the Bible
  becomes alive, prayer becomes vital, your witness
  becomes effective and obedience becomes a joy. Then,
  as a result of your obedience in these areas, your faith
  grows and you become more mature in your spiritual
  life.⁴

Great stuff! The Holy Spirit is all of this and more. And having brought us to this point, I want to make an emphatic and
very dogmatic statement. *The single greatest key to eternal success in
any Christian endeavor is allowing the full work of the Holy Spirit in and
through us.* This is true for our personal growth and development,
and it is certainly true concerning all ministry. In spite of this,
He is largely ignored and taken for granted.

If we are to become skilled watchmen, we must become
increasingly led and instructed by the Holy Spirit. Watchmen
watch Him! He was Christ's helper, and He must be ours as well.

Jesus was filled with, led, empowered and anointed by the Holy Spirit (see Luke 4). Acts 10:38 again says Christ derived His power from the Holy Spirit, and our power flows from the same source—the Holy Spirit (see Acts 1:8).

In a seminary missions class, Herbert Jackson told how, as a new missionary, he was assigned a car that would not start without a push.

After pondering his problem, he devised a plan. He went to the school near his home, got permission to take some children out of class, and had them push his car off. As he made his rounds, he would either park on a hill or leave his car running. He used this ingenious procedure for two years.

Ill health forced the Jackson family to leave, and a new missionary came to that station. When Jackson proudly began to explain his arrangement for getting the car started, the new man began looking under the hood. Before the explanation was complete, the new missionary interrupted, "Why Dr. Jackson, I believe the only trouble is this loose cable." He gave the cable a twist, stepped into the car, pushed the switch, and to Jackson's astonishment, the engine roared to life.

For two years needless trouble had become routine. The power was there all the time. Only a loose connection kept Jackson from putting the power to work.

J. B. Phillips paraphrases Ephesians 1:19-20, "How tremendous is the power available to us who believe in God." When we make firm our connection with the Holy Spirit, His life and power flow through us.[5]

Our Battle Partner

There are two references in Scripture to the Holy Spirit's being our Helper. One is the aforementioned verse, John 16:7: "But I tell you the truth, it is to your advantage that I go away; for if I do not go away, the *Helper* shall not come to you; but if I go, I will send Him to you." Here the word is *parakletos*, which literally means "called to another's side to aid, help or support."[6] While often used to describe a legal advocate or attorney, it is not limited to this, but includes any and every means of helping.

Another interesting use of the term *parakletos* was in ancient warfare. "Greek soldiers went into battle in pairs so when the enemy attacked, they could draw together back-to-back, covering each other's blind side. One's battle partner was the *paraclete*."[7]

Yes, our greatest partner in battle is the Holy Spirit! As Samson of old, we become more than conquerors when He is our strength.

The Amplified Bible uses no less than seven terms to describe or translate the concept of the Holy Spirit as our *paraclete*: "Comforter, Counselor, Helper, Advocate, Intercessor, Strengthener, Standby." The point is simple yet broad. The Holy Spirit has been sent to help us in every aspect of our life and ministry. *He is the key to success!* We must lean heavily on Him, watchmen.

The second passage which refers to the Holy Spirit's helping us is Romans 8:26, "And in the same way the Spirit also *helps* our weakness; for we do not know how to pray as we should, but the Spirit Himself intercedes for us with groanings too deep for words" (italics mine). The Greek word is *sunantilambonomai*. It is a compound word made up of three words. *Sun* means "together with"; *anti*, "against"; and *lambano*, "to take hold of."[8] Putting them together, a very literal meaning of the word would be "take hold of together with against."

How's that for help?!

In situations where we're experiencing difficulty in obtaining results, the Holy Spirit wants to take hold of the situation with us, adding His strength to ours. He also wants to help or take hold with us by directing us how to pray "for we know not what we should pray for as we ought" (Rom. 8:26, *KJV*).

Although the context of 2 Corinthians 12:9 is not prayer, praying in the Spirit is perhaps the greatest example of when His strength is made complete in our weaknesses. Realizing our weaknesses and our inability to produce results causes us to look to Him for help. If we allow Him to pray through us, He will take hold together with us. We just have to believe that when the Holy Spirit takes hold, something is going to move!

Please notice that both the word "helps" and its literal definition "takes hold *together* with against" imply not that He is doing it *for* us but *with* us. In other words, this isn't something the Holy Spirit is simply doing in us, with or without our participation. No, we involve Him by praying in the Spirit, which is actually allowing Him to pray through us.

As I shared in *Intercessory Prayer*, several years ago my wife, Ceci, developed a pain in her abdomen. An ovarian cyst was discovered, and she was advised to have surgery. However, her doctor was a believer and, being confident this was not life threatening, agreed to give us two months to pursue healing through prayer.

We prayed for Ceci with every biblical method we knew of: laying on of hands, elders anointing her with oil, the prayer of agreement, etc. No change in her condition occurred, and I realized we were going to have to obtain this healing through perseverance and laying hold by faith (see 1 Tim. 6:12). That, by the way, is the way most answers to prayer come—not as instant miracles, but through fighting the fight of faith and patience. This perseverance is part of the watchman concept of laying siege. Most of the time we need this long-term siege mentality. For a fuller treatment of why persistence is needed in prayer, I strongly encourage you to read chapter 12 in my book *Intercessory Prayer*.

I felt I needed to spend an hour a day praying for Ceci. I began my prayer times by stating my reason for approaching the Father. Then I referred to the Scriptures on which I was basing my petition. I would quote them, thanking the Father for His Word and Jesus for providing healing. This usually took no more than five or six minutes. I prayed in the Spirit for the remainder of the hour. This siege went on for a month.

After a couple of weeks of this, one afternoon the Lord showed me a picture as I was praying in the Spirit. I saw myself holding this cyst in my hand, squeezing the life out of it. I did not yet know that the literal meaning of "helps" in Romans 8 was "taking hold of together with against," but the Holy Spirit was teaching me a wonderful truth.

I knew, of course, that I couldn't really get my hands on the cyst; but He was showing me that as I allowed Him to pray through me, He was taking hold with me against the thing. Obviously, it was His power making the difference.

It sort of reminds me of the mouse and the elephant who were best friends. They hung out together all the time, the mouse riding on the elephant's back. One day they crossed a wooden bridge, causing it to bow, creak and sway under their combined weight. After they were across, the mouse, impressed over their ability to make such an impact, said to the elephant, "We sure shook up that bridge, didn't we?"

Kind of reminds me of some of our advertisements and testimonials. You'd think He was the mouse and we were the elephant. (Maybe that's why we don't shake many bridges.)

After seeing the picture of myself squeezing the life out of the cyst, I asked Ceci if there was any change in her condition. "Yes, the pain is decreasing," she informed me.

The doctor's response was "If the pain is decreasing, the cyst must be shrinking. Keep doing whatever it is you're doing." The siege was working.

I tried hard to make sure I wasn't conjuring up any mental images, but twice more the Holy Spirit showed me this same picture. Each time the cyst was smaller. The last of them, which was the third time over-all, was about a month into the process. In the picture the cyst was about the size of a quarter, and as I prayed, it vanished in my hand. I knew the Lord was letting me know the work was finished. Even though Ceci said there was still a very small amount of discomfort, I could not bring myself to pray about it any further. I knew it was done.

The Holy Spirit has much to say if we learn to listen. He is the means to all revelation from God.

Three days later she informed me that all the pain and discomfort was gone. The subsequent ultrasound confirmed what we already knew in our hearts—no more cyst! The watchman anointing was a major part of this wonderful healing.

THE MANY ROLES OF THE HOLY SPIRIT

One further reference and some amplified definitions will give us even more insight into the role of our Helper. Second Corinthians 13:14 says, "The grace of the Lord Jesus Christ, and the love of God, and the *fellowship of the Holy Spirit*, be with you all." The word "fellowship" here is *koinonia* and is rich with meaning, as can be seen in the following definitions:

Fellowship; Communion

The word *koinonia* implies that the Holy Spirit wants intimacy with us. This very word is used in 1 Corinthians 10:16 to describe the Lord's table, the bread and the wine. This is appropriate since it is the Lord's shed blood and broken body that brings us into covenantal, intimate *communion* with Him.

The Holy Spirit wants to commune with us. He has much to say if we learn to listen. He is the means to all revelation from God. He is the Teacher. He is a part of the Godhead we're to be in relationship with. Let Him fellowship and commune with you.

At times His fellowship with you requires no speaking. Some communion is heart to heart.

Rowell provides this illustration:

In his book *Good Morning Merry Sunshine*, Chicago Tribune columnist Bob Greene chronicles his infant daughter's first year of life. When little Amanda began crawling, he records: "This is something I'm having trouble getting used to. I will be in bed reading a book or watching TV. And I will look down at the foot of the bed and there will be Amanda's head staring back at me.

"Apparently I've become one of the objects that fascinates her. . . . It's so strange. After months of having to go to her, now she is choosing to come to me. I don't know quite how to react. All I can figure is that she likes the idea of coming in and looking at me. She doesn't expect anything in return. I'll return her gaze and in a few minutes she'll decide she wants to be back in the living room and off she'll crawl again."

The simple pleasure of looking at the one you love is

what we enjoy each time we worship God and bask in His presence.[9]

At times I crawl up to God for a look. Just knowing He is looking back is enough. At other times He shares His heart while I'm gazing.

There is an amazing picture of this sort of intimacy in the following Scriptures:

- For the devious are an abomination to the LORD; but He is *intimate* with the upright (Prov. 3:32, italics mine).
- The *secret* of the LORD is for those who fear Him, and He will make them know His covenant (Ps. 25:14, italics mine).

The words "secret" and "intimacy" are translated from the same Hebrew word *cowd*, which means "couch, cushion or pillow."[10] The picture is one of two intimate friends seated on a couch, sharing their most intimate thoughts with one another. Or perhaps of a wife and husband sharing a pillow, conversing intimately.

"Do you really think God wants that kind of relationship, Sheets?" you may be asking.

Absolutely! Abraham was His friend. David was a man after God's heart (see 1 Sam. 13:14). If that didn't mean so much to the Lord, why did He share it three times in Scripture? Enoch walked with Him until God took him on to heaven (see Gen. 5:22,24). The disciples were called His friends (see John 15:15).

We can be His friends, too.

I was ministering in Toronto several months ago. My last morning there, as I was packing my bags and thinking about my final session, I was also visiting with the Holy Spirit. I wasn't in intercession, and it wasn't during my quiet time. It was simply communing while working, sharing some of my inner thoughts with Him, much the same way I might have done with my wife had she been there.

Suddenly He spoke to me. It was as natural and matter of fact as if two friends were sharing their hearts. "Japan is really on My heart this morning," the Holy Spirit said.

This surprised me because I've never thought about God's having one place on His heart more than others. I've always figured He had *every place* on His heart all the time. And the phrase "on My heart" surprised me as well. It was more than on His mind, this was something deeper—very important to Him. I felt as though He were letting me into His very heart.

He then said to me, "I must have Japan. It is a gate to Asia and I must have it. There is tremendous warfare over the nation right now. Would you pray for Japan this morning in your session?"

How do you like that?! Not a command, "Pray for Japan," but a question, "Would you?" He was *asking* me!

"Of course we will, Holy Spirit," I said. "We would be honored to do that." And we did! Such an anointing and burden came upon the assembly—tears, travail, intense intercession. It went on for about 45 minutes, at which time I had to leave for the airport. They continued—how long I do not know.

God brought tremendous insight to us in that session of how to pray for Japan. He spoke to us prophetically some promises to lay hold of and to declare over the nation. It was glorious. I'm told that somehow many believers in Japan have heard about it and been very encouraged. Japan will be saved! (I'm not implying this only because of our prayers that day. I simply have strong faith concerning this nation.)

This watching and subsequent intercession was born out of fellowship with the Holy Spirit.

Sharing Together; Participation in or with Something or Someone

The Holy Spirit wants to share His strength, power, wisdom and information with us. He is desirous of participating with us in life's endeavors. He certainly wants to participate with us in our prayer lives.

Paul Grabill interviewed Eric Harrah, who, prior to his conversion to Christ in 1997, had been the second largest abortion provider in the United States. Harrah recalls how the supernatural working of the Holy Spirit through Steve Srupar played a part in his decision:

> "A week before I gave my life back to Christ, we were sitting at a restaurant and Steve said he wanted to confirm three things the Holy Spirit had revealed to him. He asked me if the name John meant anything to me; I replied it was my grandfather's name. He asked if I knew a girl in a plaid outfit and a white shirt; I knew that was my sister because my grandfather had a picture of her in that school outfit. I wasn't too impressed, though, because everyone knew my grandfather and that I had a sister.
>
> "Then he said the Holy Spirit had revealed to him a plate that had blue pills with white bands on it, and wanted to know if that meant anything to me. I denied it at first, but later called him and told him its significance. About a week before, after coming home with joint pains, I decided to take some pain medication. As I went to take one of my blue pills with the white band, I said to myself, *Enough is enough—tonight is a good night to die.* I dumped all the blue pills onto a plate; then got my other medication and dumped all of them on the plate too. As I started to put the first pill in my mouth, my dog

barked and looked at me as if to say, Who's going to take care of me? I knew nobody would, so I put the pills back in their containers.

"It was amazing to me that the Holy Ghost revealed such details to him. I knew it was time to give in."

One reason God gives us the power of the Holy Spirit is to help us win lost people to Christ.[11]

Watchmen learn to *partner* with Him, and partnership with the Holy Spirit causes their prayer success rate to climb significantly!

Distribution; Impart

The Holy Spirit desires to *distribute*, or *impart*, to us all that we need to function well in life and certainly as watchmen. This verse, 2 Corinthians 13:14, is saying, "May the Holy Spirit impart to you," "May He distribute to you," of His vast resources and gifts.

I love it when the Holy Spirit distributes revelation to me as I study His Word. I then take great joy in distributing it to others.

I find it very fulfilling when, through the power of the Holy Spirit, I am used to impart a spiritual gift or perhaps power for healing to another person. Paul spoke of this in Romans 1:11, "For I long to see you in order that I may impart some spiritual gift to you, that you may be established." He also said Timothy received spiritual gifts through impartation (see 1 Tim. 4:14 and 2 Tim. 1:6). Moses imparted to Joshua a spirit of wisdom (see Deut. 34:9).

How would a human being have the ability to impart a spiritual gift if not by the power of the Holy Spirit? Does this still happen today? Of course it does.

The Holy Spirit wants to impart to us, as watchmen, information that will help us in our prayers. Jane Hamon tells of a dream He gave to her, bringing information that helped save their church from great problems:

> I once dreamed that someone poisoned the leader of our ministry with the intent of killing him. He did not die, but became very sick. As pastors of the church, my husband and I stood up to ask for special prayer on behalf of our leader. Before we could pray, however, someone came running up and whispered in my ear that we shouldn't announce what had happened because the person who had done the poisoning was right in our church. No one's name was mentioned.
>
> When I awakened from the dream I felt concerned. I recorded the dream and began to pray about what it meant. I felt that it was indicating a spiritual attack that was coming against not only the leader, but the ministry as well and that its intent was to bring death; not only physical death, but a death of the vision as well. This death would come as a result of a poisoning of minds and would be perpetuated from within. I examined my heart right away to see if the Lord would show me anything in my heart that could be poisoning me.
>
> Before 9:00 A.M. that morning I received two phone calls. One was from one of our church intercessors who had been praying and felt that the Lord had showed him that there was a spiritual infiltration in our church and that it was trying to bring death. He specifically mentioned the name of our leader but felt that the whole church was being affected as well. The second phone call was similar, but this individual had a dream that

revealed a spirit of death coming against our church.

My dream, plus the two additional confirmations to what I felt the dream meant caused us to begin to pray as a church and war against the plans of the enemy. Since we don't wrestle against flesh and blood, but against a spiritual foe, this is where the battle was won (see Eph. 6:12).[12]

Partaking

This is a logical follow-up to the previous definition. The Holy Spirit not only wants to distribute and impart to us, He wants us to partake of Him. If we will not partake, He cannot impart. Much of what He wants to give is missed because of unbelief and ignorance.

Read the verse again with faith: "May you partake of the Holy Spirit!" What a statement! Let's draw from Him daily—strength, ability, compassion, power and an ability to watch.

Quin Sherrer tells of a friend who partook of Holy Spirit's ability to watch for her possessions:

I was rooming with Ruthie at a Christian conference when she told me how God had protected her property. One night during the church service she heard a voice: "Your house is being robbed." She tried to dismiss the thought. She'd lived in that house for thirty years and there had been no burglaries in her neighborhood. But the more she thought about it, the more it seemed to her that the inner voice she had heard was the Holy Spirit warning her.

"Lord, if our house is being robbed, please send an angel—no, Lord, send a warring angel—to frighten the burglar off." Then she began to quote Scriptures, praying for protection: "No evil will come near our dwelling place.... No weapon formed against us shall prosper...."

Sure enough, when she and her husband arrived home, their back patio door was smashed in and everything inside was in disarray—drawers open and stuff scattered everywhere. The next day, when the police officer came to get a list of the things they knew were missing, all they had to report was one pillow case. He told them that's what a burglar usually takes to stash the valuables. "As far as we can tell nothing is missing—not even my good gold jewelry," Ruthie told him.

He looked around at her china, silver, gold vases. "With all these beautiful things, I don't understand why you weren't robbed blind. Something obviously frightened away the intruder. He left in a hurry," the policeman said.

Two other houses in her neighborhood were robbed that night. Ruthie is sure God sent a warring angel of protection, as she had prayed and asked Him to do.[13]

Partake of the Holy Spirit's love and communion, yes. But also draw on His supernatural ability to protect that which belongs to you.

Partnership; Companionship

What an amazing thought! The Holy Spirit is saying to us, "I want to be your partner and companion. Allow Me to partner with you in your prayer life. Let me be your companion as you walk through the Word each day. Let me join with you in this calling to be a watchman. We can accomplish much together!"

Wow!

Bob Beckett, whom we've already mentioned as one of the Hemet, California, pastors used to impact that city, shares of many situations where the Holy Spirit supernaturally gave the correct strategy for prayer. Until they learned to listen for that strategy, allowing the Holy Spirit to be their watchman partner, the fruit was very limited. Beckett says:

> We knew the value of prayer. We knew how to bind demonic forces. We were willing to put in the time and energy. We did not have enough understanding, however, of what our enemy was doing to hold Hemet in bondage. We did not know how to aim our prayers in such a way as to destroy Satan's strongholds—fortresses that exist both in the mind and in particular locations.
>
> The first thing we had to do was find out the Lord's agenda for our community. What was it He wanted us to tackle in our warfare praying? How were we to approach various problems? What was God's highest priority in our town? If we wanted to see His Kingdom come and His will be done in Hemet, we needed to know what His will was.[14]

As they grew in their ability to follow the Holy Spirit's directives, things began to change rapidly. Beckett goes on to say:

> An understanding of "smart bomb praying"—prayers armed with warheads of specific information regarding issues of darkness within our community—moved us into strategic-level intercession, delivering smart bomb prayers on behalf of a geographical location (in our case, Hemet). And as The Dwelling Place [our church] moved toward accurate, strategic-level praying, we began to find

THE WATCHMAN'S ALLY 163

out what really—and I mean *really*—was going on in our city.

The Lord revealed more and more to us as we prayed. Because we knew where problems had the greatest grip and why those areas were more affected, we learned what we were hitting with our prayers. After a while, when we prayed, we could go back and evaluate our progress. If we did not see significant changes, we knew to go back and pray some more.

Eventually we started seeing breakthroughs in our community. Nothing has fulfilled me more as a pastor than watching this city I love so dearly become more infiltrated with the Kingdom of God. God allowed us to arrive at the place where we could employ smart bomb strategies in our intercession.[15]

Smart bomb strategies in intercession come from the smart Holy Spirit, not smart Christians. We don't know enough to function as watchmen without Him. Let your Prayer Partner help!

Time Never Wasted

Koinonia means not only partnership but companionship as well. Let me say, without fear of error, God longs for and craves companionship with us. That's why He made us. It's why Jesus came—to redeem us back into relationship with Him. Let it happen.

In *The Effective Father*, Gordon MacDonald shares a story that exemplifies the nature of companionship:

It is said of Boswell, the famous biographer of Samuel Johnson, that he often referred to a special day in his childhood when his father took him fishing. The day was fixed in his mind, and he often reflected upon many things his father had taught him in the course of their fishing experience together.

After having heard of that particular excursion so often, it occurred to someone much later to check the journal that Boswell's father kept and determine what had been said about the fishing trip from the parental perspective. Turning to that date, the reader found only one sentence entered: "Gone fishing today with my son; a day wasted."[16]

Do you consider time spent with Him wasted? He doesn't! And neither do wise watchmen.

Notes
1. Spiros Zodhiates, *Hebrew-Greek Key Study Bible—New American Standard,* rev. ed. (Chattanooga, TN: AMG Publishers, 1990), p. 4851.
2. Craig Brian Larson, *Choice Contemporary Stories and Illustrations for Preachers, Teachers, and Writers* (Grand Rapids, MI: Baker Book House, 1998), p. 54.
3. Robert Heidler, *Experiencing the Spirit* (Ventura, CA: Renew Books, 1998), p. 35, citing Bill Bright.
4. Ibid.
5. Craig Brian Larson, *Illustrations for Preaching and Teaching* (Grand Rapids, MI: Baker Book House, 1993), p. 182.
6. James Strong, *The New Strong's Exhaustive Concordance of the Bible* (Nashville, TN: Thomas Nelson Publishers, 1990), ref. no. 3875.
7. Edward K. Rowell, *Fresh Illustrations for Preaching and Teaching* (Grand Rapids, MI: Baker Book House, 1997), p. 110.
8. Strong, *New Strong's Exhaustive Concordance of the Bible,* ref. no. 4878.
9. Rowell, *Fresh Illustrations for Preaching and Teaching,* p. 224.
10. Strong, *New Strong's Exhaustive Concordance of the Bible,* ref. no. 5475.
11. Larson, *Choice Contemporary Stories and Illustrations,* pp. 123, 124.
12. Jane Hamon, *Dreams and Visions* (Santa Rosa Beach, FL: Christian International, 1997), pp. 98, 99.

13. Quin Sherrer, *Listen, God Is Speaking to You* (Ann Arbor, MI: Servant Publications, 1999), pp. 148, 149.

14. Bob Beckett, *Commitment to Conquer* (Grand Rapids, MI: Chosen Books, 1997), pp. 34, 35.

15. Ibid., p. 35.

16. Larson, *Illustrations for Preaching and Teaching*, p. 83.

WATCHMEN AREN'T WATCHDOGS

Chapter Ten

THE DAY MY DOG TP'D THE YARD

Mercedes. I have one. No, not a car or a sports utility van—she's a dog. A big boxer my wife and daughters named Mercedes. I just called her "One More." We already had two small dogs, Cocoa and Missy. We felt "led" to get a big dog because the rural area we recently moved to has coyotes and foxes, and our two small dogs look like coyote and fox food.

So along came Mercedes. The protector! Man's best friend. (Excuse me, ladies, *"People's* best friend.") Cocoa and Missy's bodyguard.

It didn't take long for Mercedes to establish herself as the *tormenting, "I'm still a puppy—let me see what I can get into"* bodyguard.

The two small dogs begged us to get rid of her. We could see it in their eyes. Now that she is nine months old and 65 pounds, they plead with us to excommunicate her, not fully understanding the eating habits of coyotes and foxes. Well, maybe they do. Perhaps they see it as a way out.

Mercedes loves to assert her dominance over the smaller dogs. One of the ways she does this is standing over them—literally. She straddles them, positioning herself over and around them, stating in essence, "I'm in charge here." Of course, she doesn't hurt them. She doesn't have to; they obey her quickly. Once in a while she sits on them lightly, just to emphasize her dominance.

The other day she did it to me. I was lying face down on the floor when she came, straddled me and sat down with her posterior on mine. Fixing a proud, assertive look on her face, she stared from me, to Ceci, to the kids. We all knew what she was saying, "I'm in charge here. Don't think for a minute that you are the head of this household."

The other day she was on the roof with me—yes, the roof. I was hanging Christmas lights and went through Hannah's bedroom window to get to the roof. The next thing I knew, there she was, inspecting my work and giving me one of those "Do you know what you're doing?" looks. You'd think she would have been scared. No way. I had to chase her all over the roof to capture and remove her. I'm now known in the neighborhood as the guy who chases dogs on roofs.

Ceci and the girls are finally taking her to obedience school. I think it's working—they came home barking (bear with my humor).

One day Mercedes TP'd (toilet papered) the yard of our previous home. No, I'm not kidding. She TP'd my yard! I saw this trail of toilet paper leaving the powder room (for all you guys, that's a half-bathroom kept clean all the time for guests), leading to the patio doors. Because the backyard was fenced, we sometimes left the door open so the dogs (Cocoa; Missy; and Mercedes, the Tormenting Protector) could wander in and out.

It was beautiful. You wouldn't think a dog could make such designs: figure eights, donuts, stripes and much more—real works of art. My neighbors couldn't believe a dog really did it, that is, until they saw her proudly standing guard over her work. She wouldn't let me clean it up for days.

I've had my church TP'd a few times. Well, not exactly, not with toilet paper. But believe me, I've had some major sheep messes to clean up. I have a sign in my office: "TP Happens." Some of those messy sheep were intercessors. They would probably consider themselves watchmen. Watchdogs would be more accurate. Most of my intercessors are wonderful, and I certainly don't throw out the good with the bad; but nonetheless, I've known some real, as I heard one person state it, "granola" intercessors: fruits, flakes and nuts.

Some so-called watchmen see demons behind every tree, have visions daily and dream "prophetic" dreams every night. They're downright scary and they give true watchman intercessors a bad name. My advice to pastors and leaders is not to reject the prophetic, including watching intercessors, just because of a few strange ones. In spite of the strange ones, I agree with Bob Beckett: "It is a wise pastor who understands and encourages the intercessors of the congregation to use their God-given gifts to help him or her fulfill the position of gatekeeper."[1]

SENSIBLE WATCHMEN

The purpose of this chapter is to give practical instruction that will help keep us balanced and make our gifts a blessing. As watchmen, we must ask ourselves at least three major questions when processing information that comes to us supernaturally.

- Is the information from God? (In other words, we must discern the source.)
- What does it mean? (We must interpret the information correctly.)
- What do I do with it? (We must determine the course of action.)

Whether it comes in the form of voices, impressions, visions or dreams, all information must be carefully tested. Perhaps you are considering a dream. The first obvious round of questions consists of these: Was it given by the Holy Spirit, or did it originate in the subconscious mind? It may have even come from a demon. How can we be certain a revelation, warning or prompting is from the Holy Spirit and not our own imagination or fears?

Dr. Freda Lindsay tells of an important dream from the Holy Spirit, which was almost overlooked:

After paying out the property we had purchased behind Christian Center, we were now ready to launch into the construction of the headquarters for Christ For The Nations and the printing building. Actually, we were overcrowded in every department to say the least.

Throughout the Bible there are instances where God spoke to individuals through dreams. One such experience came to me the night of November 13, 1968. I dreamed that the men who were constructing our new headquarters building were placing it at the wrong end of the property. After a bit I woke up, fell asleep again and dreamed virtually the same dream. Again I woke up, fell asleep and dreamed the same dream the third time.

When morning came I couldn't figure out what it was all about, as I was sure the contractor knew exactly which end of the property to put the building on. And so I dismissed it from my mind.

We were leaving in two days to take a tour group to Israel. The day before leaving, Gordon and I drove over to the building site. As I stood there looking at the pegs outlining the location of the building, I was surprised to see that it was at the opposite end of the property from where we had planned it. I mentioned this to Gordon and he calmly remarked, "Oh, these are no doubt just preliminary stakes and have nothing to do with the location of the building."

Suddenly recalling the three dreams I had had the night before, I said to Gordon, "Let's talk to the foreman."

To our amazement he confirmed what I suspected. He had misunderstood, and was actually putting the building at the opposite end of the property from where we wanted it. This would have caused no end of problems as we needed the print shop loading docks next to the street. The warning dream had come just in time![2]

A mistake that seemed too outlandish to be true was, indeed, being made. Had Dr. Lindsay not given credence to the dream, great problems would have resulted.

While we don't want to say every impression that comes to us is from God, we also don't want to ignore promptings of the Spirit out of naivete or fear of being wrong. First Thessalonians 5:21 instructs us to "Examine everything carefully; hold fast to that which is good." The word "examine" is *dokimazo*, which means to put something to the test or put it on trial.³ The context is receiving supernatural information. The preceding verses warn not to quench the Spirit or despise prophecy. The Holy Spirit's balanced instruction to us is, "Don't be afraid of the subjective realm of supernatural revelation. At the same time, don't buy everything that comes along. Test it."

Acid Tests

There are three basic ways we judge revelation:

The Scriptures

The Word of God is the absolute authority in the life of a Christian. Any alleged revelation that contradicts the Bible is not from the Holy Spirit. For example, if someone told me God led him or her to leave their current spouse in order to marry another—and they have—I would know immediately they were deceived. The Holy Spirit who wrote Matthew 19:6 wouldn't contradict it: "Consequently they are no longer two, but one flesh. What therefore God has joined together, let no man separate."

Beth Alves says in her book *Becoming a Prayer Warrior*, "Satan does not want you to hear God's voice because your partnership with the Lord can wreak havoc on his kingdom."[4] She goes on to share 13 excellent guidelines to hearing the voice of God and eight ways to test what is heard. My purpose in this chapter isn't to thoroughly teach how to hear from God. It would be presumptive of me, if not foolish, to give such a cursory treatment to such an important subject. My intent is simply to share a few guidelines and boundaries for us as watchmen.

I would strongly encourage you to study books such as *Becoming a Prayer Warrior* by Beth Alves, *Listen, God Is Speaking to You* by Quin Sherrer and *The Voice of God* by Cindy Jacobs, as these are wonderfully complete and balanced teachings on how to hear God speak. We often don't want to take the time to do something such as this, but to ignore this responsibility is a sure way to create problems. The following story is all too true:

> In *The Essential Calvin and Hobbes* by Bill Watterson, the cartoon character Calvin says to his tiger friend, Hobbes, "I feel bad that I called Susie names and hurt her feelings. I'm sorry I did it."
>
> "Maybe you should apologize to her," Hobbes suggests.
>
> Calvin ponders this for a moment and replies, "I keep hoping there's a less obvious solution."[5]

Some messes made by irresponsible Christians have obvious solutions. While the Bible is the number one measure by which we judge all information, there are times, however, when Scripture will not specifically answer the question of whether or not a revelation is of God. Still, the information must harmonize with the general wisdom, ways and character of God in the Word. An example of such a situation is when we receive a caution concerning another person.

In these types of situations, where there is no direct Scripture to validate a word, we should ask ourselves questions such as:

- Does this person bringing the warning seem to have a critical spirit? The Holy Spirit never aligns Himself with the accuser of the brethren.

WATCHMEN AREN'T WATCHDOGS   173

- Does this person have a proven track record in being able to discern things such as this?
- Is there a legitimate reason why the Holy Spirit would warn me about this person? If there is no potential for involvement with an individual, the Holy Spirit probably wouldn't give information that would affect my trust or acceptance of them.
- Is the warning confirmed by what I perceive in my heart?
- Has anyone else confirmed this caution?

We can see that even where Scripture doesn't give literal answers to our questions, the principles and wisdom it contains are always applicable.

Wise Counsel
The second way of determining the source of information is wise counsel. If we are walking in biblical principles of relationship and accountability, God always has individuals in our lives that can give us sound advice. It is never wise to act on subjective revelation without seeking the wisdom of others, especially if the Scriptures don't address in a literal way what is revealed.

We are all susceptible to prejudices, traditions, past paradigms, misinterpretation of Scripture and, yes, even demonic spirits, all of which can cause us to be misled. True humility is the willingness to allow others to help judge our leanings, leadings and revelations.

I was given a word of warning from a supposed watchman a few years back about another person. I was told, "That individual is a witch. You need to get her out of the church."

I do experience a lot of spiritual warfare, and I know I've had witches in our services, trying to cause problems. Of course, I don't like this and I certainly don't want any to infiltrate our church, becoming "plants" working against us behind the scenes. I did not bear witness with this warning, however, and absolutely didn't want to falsely accuse a sincere person. I have seen people terribly bruised by false accusations of this sort.

What did I do? I sought wise counsel and discreetly asked other discerning people to pray with me. We decided the Lord was telling us this person wasn't a witch, and we disregarded the warning word. As it turns out, she is a wonderful, sincere Christian with a very real, serving heart. Wise counsel is invaluable.

Confirmation

The third way we judge whether or not a revelation or warning is from the Holy Spirit is by asking God for confirmation. I received a strong warning from an intercessor several years ago that a certain individual in ministry was going to die unless steps were taken to help him. The first question I had to answer was, "Is this serious warning from God?"

I asked God for confirmation. Within a week, two more individuals gave me the same warning about the same person, and none of the three people had spoken with the others or heard about their warnings. I had my confirmations.

On another occasion, a prophetic intercessor told me she felt very strongly that I was wrong in rejecting a certain invitation to speak. God confirmed this person's word to me within a week through two other watchmen telling me the same thing. None of them had spoken with each other or had knowledge of the others' warnings. I took the meeting!

This, unlike the death warning, wasn't a life-or-death situation, but it certainly was a word that kept me from missing

God's plan for my ministry. Tremendous fruit resulted from that meeting, which would have been missed had I not received and heeded the warning and confirmations.

WHAT DOES THIS MEAN?

After we have confirmed that information given to us is indeed from God, we need to ask ourselves, *What does this mean?*

- Is the information symbolic or literal?
- Is this something happening currently or a warning about the future?
- And often in order to determine the proper meaning, we must ask ourselves, *Am I the one who should interpret this information?*

Symbolic or Literal
I recently had a dream, which I knew was from the Holy Spirit. It involved President Clinton, my state of Colorado and myself. It isn't necessary to share the details, but it had symbolic aspects to it and the dream seemed very important. Because I do not feel gifted at interpreting dreams, I asked others to help me and received what I believe was an accurate interpretation. There is wisdom in asking for help in understanding information given to us by the Spirit.

I mentioned previously three warnings concerning the potential death of a fellow minister. One of the warnings came in the form of a detailed dream. In the dream this individual fell into what appeared to be a mud puddle but was actually a deep pit. The only part of his body sticking out of the pit was a foot with a wool sock on it.

Not feeling competent to fully understand the dream and its symbolism myself, I asked for help. I knew that three separate warnings surely indicated the accuracy and seriousness of this situation. The person interpreting the dream knew from several details it was a warning about death, but also drew significant insight from the picture of the wool sock. The man in danger was a pastor, but the wool sock was a reminder that he was also a sheep, not just a shepherd, and needed to be carefully pastored through this time. This was done, the man's life was saved and I am pleased to say he is well and still in ministry today.

Relating this to the above questions, I first determined that I was *not* the person to interpret some of the information. Secondly, we concluded that the warning was definitely for the present. And thirdly, there was symbolic information, which needed to be interpreted.

Correct Application of Time, Person and Place

Sometimes watchmen receive words from the Holy Spirit and have difficulty discerning the timing. I have received warnings from them about situations they thought to be current, which in reality were concerning the future. Had we not discerned this, we would have discarded the warnings altogether because they made no sense at the time they were issued.

One such event several years ago involved an intercessor encouraging me that "the strife among our leadership team was going to be taken care of by the Lord." She assured me she was praying about it and had peace that God was intervening.

I wasn't aware of any strife among our team members at the time and was confused. I also grew somewhat alarmed because she was so adamant and is usually accurate. Upon quizzing my staff—even pressing the issue—they all assured me, and finally convinced me, that there were no problems among us.

The Holy Spirit, however, showed us that actually what she was discerning by the Spirit was a future but imminent attack by Satan to divide us. We were then able to pray against it and be alert, watching for it. The attack did come, but it wasn't successful because of the warning of the Holy Spirit and preventive prayer.

I'm certain many warnings from the Holy Spirit are not heeded simply because, like the above story, they didn't make sense at the time or were not properly interpreted. These two things can also result in distrust between the giver and the recipient of the warning.

> **Many warnings from the Holy Spirit are not heeded simply because they didn't make sense at the time or were not properly interpreted.**

I experienced another situation in which a lady believed she was alerted that adultery existed in a minister's life. When praying for this minister, she kept hearing the word "adultery." As it turned out, the minister wasn't involved in adultery at all, but Satan had a plan in place to try to snare him in this area. It was exposed and unsuccessful. God was alerting her to what the enemy was *planning*, not what the pastor was *doing*, so she could pray against it.

It is easy to see how words such as these could be misinterpreted and cause great confusion and serious problems. They must be handled very carefully and often with the help of mature leaders.

What to Do with the Information

The last questions that need to be answered when a watchman believes he or she has received information from the Lord are the following:

- What do I do with this information?
- Do I tell anyone else?
- Do I inform leaders?
- Do I alert the person(s) involved?
- Do I simply pray and say nothing?

There have been instances when intercessors came to me with warnings I wish they had never shared. Had they simply prayed for me and not distracted me with the information, it would have been much more beneficial.

For example, there is spiritual warfare happening most of the time in a church or ministry that is making a true impact against the enemy. Satan relentlessly seeks to distract, discourage and destroy what they are doing. So when a watchman comes to me with the warning "Pastor, I feel there is spiritual warfare taking place against us at this time," my first thought is usually *Of course there is.*

I really don't want to be bothered with general statements such as this all the time. The watchmen are probably perceiving correctly, but they do not need to burden me with the information. The Holy Spirit is most likely trying to awaken them to pray against the attacks.

There are other times when leaders definitely need to be informed. On one occasion, I received a warning during a Wednesday evening service that there was spiritual warfare coming against us. I thanked the person that gave the warning and ho-hummed in my mind. Then a second person came with the same warning. I still wasn't too alarmed, but I thought that now it might merit being brought before the congregation for prayer.

When I mentioned it, not with any real gravity, another person in the service raised his hand and asked permission to speak. I knew him well enough to allow him to share and he informed us, "I received a call from a friend in another city today who told me he felt like our church was coming into a major attack of warfare."

My ho-hum turned into an uh-oh. Three warnings in one day, including one from a person in another city, were enough to convince me that this was a major attack. We went into immediate prayer.

I recall the meeting very well. It turned into a very precious time of intercession, but it was also a spiritual bonding among our congregation. Before the night was over, many of them formed a circle around the leadership team and prayed a strong barrier of protection around us.

The attack of the enemy failed and God turned the situation into something positive for our fellowship. What Satan meant for division and disruption became unifying and edifying.

Often watchmen also need to decide whether to alert other intercessors or just to pray themselves. Much damage can come if certain information is shared with immature or indiscreet people. Any information that would damage another's reputation or bring division to a group of people should only be disclosed to those with the God-given responsibility of dealing with it. And information that is unproven or unconfirmed should only be shared with responsible leaders and then only after much prayer.

Cindy Jacobs's book *Possessing the Gates of the Enemy* is an excellent watchman resource. She makes the following point concerning this issue:

Pray that God will teach you the proper time and place to sound the alarm. God reveals to intercessors the intimate needs of those for whom we intercede. This is a precious trust. The things God shares with us are not to be told to others. Many prayer groups are nothing more than spiritual gossip sessions. If God reveals another person's weaknesses to you, you need to: Ask for confirmation first to see if you have heard the need accurately. You do not want to pray amiss. If you are sure you are praying accurately, then you need to ask God whether or not to tell the person what you have learned. If you are to tell the person, then pray that God will prepare his or her heart to be receptive.

Many times you will never say anything to the persons for whom you have prayed. God will speak to them in His time and way. This is the most effective means of dealing with weaknesses in those for whom we have prayed. When God tells them they need to change, it does not cause them to feel embarrassed, rejected or wounded.

There are times to sound the alarm to others in your prayer group when you see a danger about to occur in your local church body. If this is the case, go to someone in a spiritual leadership position and share your prayer concern. Leave any further sharing in his or her hands.[6]

A watchman in our church received a word for me a few years back, which wasn't a very pleasant one to give. She struggled over whether or not to share it with me. The Lord ultimately was able to convince her she should. The word spoke of four things in my life God wanted to deal with and remove.

This intercessor didn't like giving the word, and I didn't particularly enjoy receiving it; but it was necessary. The Lord used her to do this because

- we had an established relationship of trust;
- she could be trusted to tell no one else;
- she did not have a critical, judgmental spirit, but rather came in humility, which helped enable me to receive it;
- she prays for my wife and me regularly;
- she is mature enough not to be disillusioned by weakness in a leader;
- she was bold enough—once she was certain the Holy Spirit was directing her—to bring me the word.

These were not sins of rebellion, immorality, dishonesty or anything else of that nature. They were subtle weaknesses that I couldn't even see at the time, nor could she. "I don't see these things in you," she told me. "But I feel strongly the Lord gave them to me concerning you."

I informed her that I didn't see them either, but I believed in her enough to earnestly seek the Lord concerning them. Within a month, God had showed all four of them to me. He and I have been working on them and will continue to do so, if necessary. In this case, the word needed to be shared with me, not just prayed over.

What a blessing this watchman word was to me! Had I not received it, who knows what snares the enemy might have laid for me at some point in time? Thank God for the watchman anointing and a watchman who knew what to do with it.

God has established this precious anointing and high calling in the Church. My prayer is that you will receive it and walk in it daily.

Much is at stake. Our gardens must be protected and preserved from the serpent and his demons. In the words of Nehemiah, "Do not be afraid of them; remember the Lord who is great and awesome, and fight for your brothers, your sons, your daughters, your wives, and your houses" (Neh. 4:14).

Rise up, watchmen, and take your position on the wall. There are cities to be protected, people to be covered and a harvest to be reaped and preserved.

The grandstands of heaven are filled with a great cloud of witnesses, cheering us on as we press toward the mark. Some have paid in blood for the truth we now enjoy and for the incredible spiritual momentum we have had handed to us as a generation.

We must not fail them or the precious Lamb who paid for it all. And we need not fail, if we answer the call. Pick up the sword, watchmen!

Notes

1. Bob Beckett, *Commitment to Conquer* (Grand Rapids, MI: Chosen Books, 1997), p. 151.
2. Mrs. Gordon Lindsay, *My Diary Secrets* (Dallas, TX: Christ For The Nations, 1976), pp. 192, 193.
3. James Strong, *The New Strong's Exhaustive Concordance of the Bible* (Nashville, TN: Thomas Nelson Publishers, 1990), ref. no. 1381.
4. Elizabeth Alves, *Becoming a Prayer Warrior* (Ventura, CA: Renew Books, 1998), p. 73.
5. Edward K. Rowell, *Fresh Illustrations for Preaching and Teaching* (Grand Rapids, MI: Baker Book House, 1997), p. 26.
6. Cindy Jacobs, *Possessing the Gates of the Enemy* (Tarrytown, NY: Chosen Books, 1991), pp. 65, 66.

ESTABLISHING A PRAYER MINISTRY*

—————— Chapter Eleven ——————

GUIDELINES FOR PRAYER

Many churches have implemented watchman prayer into the various facets of their ministries by organizing and establishing several groups of watchmen so that their church, leadership and ministries are covered in prayer. Specific intercessory teams focus on one particular group or area, such as the leaders, the church's prophetic words, special events, the various departments of the church, each service, outreaches, their cities and the nation.

Dr. Terry Teykl's books *Pray the Price, Blueprint for the House of Prayer, Making Room to Pray, How to Pray After You've Kicked the Dog* and *Mosquito on an Elephant's Rump* give outstanding insight and guidelines into establishing successful prayer in the local church. The remainder of this chapter is taken from these five excellent books. Though the following excerpts will be extremely helpful, I strongly advise that you obtain and use these invaluable books so you can study his entire teachings. Information is given at the end of the chapter for ordering these tremendous tools.

A PRAYER ROOM

Making prayer visible in our churches makes it more likely to happen and encourages more people to participate. We must do everything we can to make prayer appealing, from investing in first-class prayer materials to raising up comfortable, inviting places for people to seek God. Prayer does not have to be mercenary in order to be spiritual.[1]

One of the simplest and yet most profound things a prayer room offers is a place to be alone and still before God. It promotes humility and a visible dependence on God. Prayer rooms also generate and facilitate other prayer ideas given by the Holy Spirit to affect the whole ministry of the church in the community.[2]

Ten Reasons Your Church Needs a Prayer Room

1. One of the greatest advantages of a prayer room is that it allows us to schedule prayer in a systematic manner, making it more likely to happen. Scheduled prayer is biblical. If you read in the book of Acts, you will see

that the disciples had scheduled times of prayer—9:00 A.M. in Acts 2:15; 3:00 P.M. in Acts 3; 12:00 noon in Acts 10:9; and 3:00 P.M. in Acts 10:30. Also, scheduled prayer tends to be perspirational prayer because it is based on a conscious decision to seek God at a given time each week, not on a crisis or feeling.

2. Prayer rooms provide places where information can be gathered and prayed over, promoting agreement in prayer.

3. A prayer room provides an excellent place to keep a record of all the deeds of God in the life of the church—a reminder to thank and praise Him for all He does.

4. Prayer rooms promote ownership of the church vision and serve as tangible, visible reminders of our commitment to pray.

5. The compassion of Jesus is displayed to the community while we make a statement to them about the importance of prayer.

6. A prayer room provides a place where prayer can be practiced and matured—a training center for both corporate and individual prayer.

7. An inclusive impact is made on the church because a prayer room brings everyone to one place to pray.

8. Prayer rooms minister the presence of God to those who come, providing a place where people can be quiet and hear the voice of God. Church staff and prayer counselors can use it when a quiet, private place is needed.

9. Prayer rooms encourage soaking prayer—prolonged periods of prayer—persevering prayer. Sometimes it takes persistent prayer to reach a spiritual breakthrough. It's sobering to realize how many prayers fell just short of the mark because we gave up too soon.

10. A prayer room provides a control center for strategic prayer evangelism, for warfare and for other prayer ministries.[3]

A prayer room needs to provide privacy and be closed off from outside distractions. It should be comfortable, with a pleasant atmosphere—an inviting place to enjoy the Lord's presence. It's important that it be safely accessible 24 hours a day, with a telephone and preferably a separate outside entrance that is well-lighted and has a combination lock. It should be inspirational and should have helpful information displayed to guide people as they pray.[4]

Steps for Prayer

Mobilizing your church to pray is a *process*. There are six important steps that can mobilize prayer in your church.[5]

Step One: Pray for Prayer

- Take time to listen to God as you pray for an attitude of prayer to come upon your church.
- Pray with perseverance knowing that there will be opposition and setbacks.

Step Two: Establish Leadership Support

- It is critical to have the support of the pastor and church leadership.

- Begin praying for God to pour out a spirit of prayer in your congregation.
- Select four or five mature, respected members to serve on a prayer task force that will be responsible for planning and promoting prayer.

Step Three: Lay Groundwork

Assess your church's current prayer status.

- Are there any existing prayer ministries?
- What has been tried in the past?
- Are there any other church ministries into which organized prayer could be incorporated?
- Is there any money in the budget for prayer?

Based on where you are, lay out a master plan which includes:

- Long-term objectives that are measurable
- Short-term goals
- Action steps leading to your short-term goals

Step Four: Teach

Probably the number one stumbling block in mobilizing a church to pray is overlooking or underestimating the importance of education. Teaching the people about God's perspective on prayer is what will give your prayer ministries longevity. For prayer to become the center of church activity, the congregation must have a mind-set that makes it so, and that mind-set must be nurtured and fed.

Step Five: Implement
Offer a variety of prayer opportunities so that all in the congregation can plug in and feel enthusiastic about their participation. As you plan, consider the seven prayer temperaments and be careful not to zero in on one or two while leaving the others out.

1. Traditional–historical (Matthew)
2. Immediate–spontaneous (Mark)
3. Loving–relational (Luke)
4. Mysterious–contemplative (John)
5. Confrontational–authoritative (Paul)
6. Perceptive–visionary (Peter)
7. Ordered–structured (James)[6]

Recruit and train people to lead and serve.

- Provide necessary materials and information.

Practice term praying.

- Make sure participants always know when they are to start praying and when they are to stop.
- A definite time frame builds a sense of accomplishment and fulfillment.
- When prayer ministries are implemented, people are more apt to commit to pray again or to pray in a different area.

Step Six: Maintain and Assess

- In a highly visible way, report answers to prayer and

give feedback about what is happening through the prayer ministries to the whole congregation.

- Allow two- to three-minute testimonies on a Sunday morning.
- Regularly appreciate those who participate in the prayer ministries.
- Never stop praying for prayer and asking God for new creative ways to pray.

LEADERSHIP SUPPORT

Leadership is critical to the success of any ministry. Without it, prayer simply will not happen. The support of the pastor is crucial to the success of prayer in the church. Also, there needs to be someone besides the pastor in charge of prayer.[7]

Qualifications of a Prayer Coordinator

1. Has a strong personal prayer life
2. Is spiritually mature
3. Has the gifts of organization, encouragement, leadership and communication
4. Has a good reputation in his or her home congregation and has the confidence of church leaders and other pastors
5. Has enough time to attend key prayer events
6. Is not a pastor[8]

Responsibilities of a Prayer Coordinator

1. Oversee the intercessory prayer ministry
2. Select and enlist prayer leadership
3. Research the church's/city's current prayer ministries
4. Identify key people and enlist their support
5. Gather a wide array of resources on prayer
6. Work closely with pastors and leaders to receive prayer, vision and guidance
7. Help develop and oversee the implementation of the plan
8. Coordinate changes, programs and other activities with the church staff
9. Keep the pastor advised and request the pastor's counsel on significant matter
10. Develop an information network
11. Schedule services offering prayer, as well as orientation and training meetings
12. Schedule and conduct monthly leadership meetings
13. Encourage and promote prayer ministry throughout the church and the community[9]

Lay Groundwork

Develop a long-term prayer plan, one that is realistic and measurable. Give it a time line, assign responsibility, affirm people who pray and celebrate the results. Plans can be well thought out, bold and exciting, but if they do not match up with your church's particular giftings, they will result in unnecessary frustration and disappointment. As you begin to build your prayer ministry, take into account your current status and make sure your plans are realistic. They should challenge you a little, but not so much that failure is inevitable.[10]

Consider the following example of one of Dr. Terry Teykl's experiences:

After hosting a workshop on the value of having a prayer room, a pastor and his small but dedicated congregation were so excited about the idea, they decided to open up a spare room in their building for twenty-four hour prayer. About six months later the pastor was frustrated and confused. "The people were so excited at first, but after a month or two, interest fell off and it became a struggle. I even feel embarrassed about the fact that we failed. I don't understand what happened."

After visiting with him on the phone, I learned the church had a strong outreach to elderly people and shut-ins in their community, so I suggested that part of the prayer room be designated to reflect the needs and victories of this particular ministry. I also learned they had a core of very active youth who had a vision for their school, so I recommended they hang a special board in the prayer room where kids could leave prayer requests and praise reports, and that the youth be challenged to fill up certain hours in the schedule. Also, because it was a small congregation, they set their total goal as 40 hours of prayer each week, instead of trying to pray around the clock.

Within just a few months, all the time slots were full, testimonies were coming in and the people were excited

> Prayer must have organization and accountability to be effective. The greater the order, the more likely the ministry will last.

about the new prayer room. The textbook form of a prayer room had little appeal to keep them motivated. But when it was personalized to reflect and include those things which were important to them, they responded with excitement and a sense of purpose.[11]

Developing a plan of prayer with specific objectives in mind gives intentionality and direction to prayer. Prayer must have organization and accountability to be effective. The greater the order, the more likely the ministry will last. Corporate prayer ministries need structure to keep them on track and focused.[12] The essentials for a praying church are

- a praying leader who motivates others;
- purpose and direction—prayer plans give scope, limit and direction to intercession in the local church;
- prayer budgets—provide material for training and maintenance of the prayer ministry;
- recruitment—enlist people to pray, orchestrate sign-up methods and build accountability into the prayer ministry; and
- creativity and variety—add interest and enjoyment to prayer ministries.[13]

When organizing a quality prayer room, keep the following tips in mind. A place of prayer should, in appearance and essence, convey the supreme value of prayer in your church. Build into your plan a support base that will sustain the room for at least a year, until it is established.

1. Ask the Father, "What kind of prayer room do You want us to have?"

2. Choose people to lead in the prayer room effort.
3. Develop a statement of purpose for the prayer room. What is the definition of intercessory prayer in your church's prayer room?
4. Choose someone to coordinate the ministry.
5. Select a place in the church for the prayer center.
6. Design a floor plan or format for your prayer room. What pattern will you use? Maps and pictures can be posted on the walls to motivate prayer. A table with a card file can be used for tracking prayer requests. Stations of prayer signifying various needs and subjects can be situated throughout the room so intercessors can move throughout the room praying strategically at each station.[14]

TEACH

As you work to initiate prayer in your church, realize that you are asking people to do something that for most Americans is very difficult. We are raised to equate independence, self-reliance and confidence with strength. We believe so strongly in our own capabilities that to ask for help from anyone, even God, is like admitting defeat.[15]

As George Barna stated, "It is not enough for the pastor to pray fervently, nor is it sufficient for a leadership team to pray ardently on behalf of the congregation. Until the church owns prayer as a world-class weapon in the battle against evil and cherishes prayer as a means of intimate and constant communication with God, the turn-around efforts of a Body are severely limited, if not altogether doomed to failure."[16]

An attitude of prayer must be established.

• Build a solid, living theology of prayer (i.e., why pray?).
• Seek a vision for what God wants to do in your specific situation.
• Develop a plan to bring the vision to pass.
• Establish visible leadership for prayer.
• Become familiar with prayer resources.
• Recruit people to pray.
• Train people to pray strategically.
• Turn plans into action.[17]

Churches must be willing to pay the price for a first-class, organized, informed, visible, attractive prayer ministry. Good prayer materials cost money. Having a comprehensive prayer library is a tremendous step toward becoming a house of prayer. We need to be committed to training all of our people to pray, not just some select group who exhibit the gift of intercession. Prayer training must become an integral part of church life.[18]

The sustained effort of prayer evangelism in a prayer room invites the Holy Spirit to do at least eight important things in a church in order for it to evangelize its community:

1. The Holy Spirit imparts compassion. As we pray, the love of God for a lost world is poured into our hearts. He is the agent of love. As we pray, the Holy Spirit imparts the love that transcends technique; He overcomes our apathy and coldness of heart; and He moves us to the self-sacrifice required to build a relationship with a lost person to secure them in Christ.
2. The Holy Spirit calls us to repentance. As intercessors pray in the prayer room, corporate repentance takes

place as a work of the Spirit, beginning with the church first and then spreading outward to the community.

3. The Holy Spirit guides our outreach and gives us a relevant message for our community. When a church prays continually in a corporate manner over its vision and outreach, the Spirit initiates mission. Divine alignment in evangelism is the work of the Holy Spirit in answer to prayer.

4. The Holy Spirit empowers Christians for witness.

5. The Holy Spirit grants laborers for the harvest.

6. The Holy Spirit gives means and resourceful ideas to the church's outreaches. New methods and approaches to evangelism are the work of the Spirit.

7. The Holy Spirit adds vitality and life to existing ministries in the local church. The Spirit empowers the life of the local church to make it attractive. Corporate intercession over a church's membership can invite the Holy Spirit to cleanse us of any and all attitudes that diminish our witness for Christ.

8. In answer to prayer, the Holy Spirit will give unity and a city-wide vision for the harvest.[19]

IMPLEMENT, MAINTAIN AND ASSESS

Everyone who participates in prayer ministry needs to know the guidelines, rules and boundaries, and must be willing to submit to the leadership of the group. It's important that people understand that prayer is a discipline that can be learned. Training builds confidence and expertise in prayer. Dick

Eastman's *The Hour That Changes the World* is an excellent teaching model. Each church needs to find what will work best for them.

As people pray the Scriptures, corporate prayer becomes alive and is saved from boredom. A prayer guide can be used to lead prayer through the Word, asking God to perform His Word in specific areas. The Word of God gives vocabulary to prayer and is the prayer language of the Father. Let the Word permeate your prayer ministry.[20]

As you recruit people to pray, it is helpful to set specific goals for recruitment, such as 20 hours of prayer each week, 40 hours of prayer each week, 144 hours of prayer each week or whatever is appropriate for your situation. Here are some guidelines for successful recruiting:

1. Try to offer a variety of prayer models to appeal to different people.
2. Make everything about your prayer ministry as first-class and attractive as possible.
3. The best place to recruit is from the pulpit. People support what the pastor supports.
4. Print the purpose of the prayer room in your bulletin or newsletter, and give updates on its development.
5. Make sure your prayer recruitment emphasis does not conflict with other major events in the church.
6. Approach groups in the church, such as youth, singles', women's and men's groups—make this a church-wide emphasis.
7. Put up a sign-up board in the foyer.
8. Be organized and state very clearly the ministry objectives and requirements, including the starting date and the date it will finish—term praying.

9. Make your prayer room part of the new member orientation.

10. Emphasize special considerations that may help people feel more comfortable with the idea of signing up for prayer.

11. Use alternates and day captains to improve participation and to establish accountability.

12. Give feedback to those who pray so they can be motivated by the answers. Publish the results of prayer in your church bulletin or newsletter, or make prayer announcements from the pulpit.

13. Appreciate those who pray in visible ways.[21]

It is very important to be alert and stand guard against the inevitable attacks of Satan. Five demonic attacks are listed below with an appropriate response through prayer:

1. *Satan Wants to Bring Destruction:* Our response to this attack should be to pray God's protection over the prayer ministry. Take authority over Satan in the strong name of Jesus, binding him with the blood of our Lord.

2. *Satan Cultivates Indifference:* We can counter apathy when we ask God to raise up enough intercessors and reserves to fill each hour.

3. *Satan Works Through Enshrinement:* We can combat pride when we pray that God will never let us become more impressed with the ministry than with Him. Ask God to help us to look only to Him, giving Him the glory.

4. *Satan Wants to See Carnal Intercessors:* The solution to this subtle corruption is to pray that God will have full control over every intercessor's life.

5. *Satan Encourages Indiscretion:* Our defense is to pray that
   God will cause us to set a guard over our mouths.
   Nothing will destroy the intercessory prayer ministry
   as quickly as gossiping about people's problems and
   needs. Do not share these needs with anyone once you
   leave the prayer room unless you have permission to
   do so. This matter is critical. The effects are disastrous
   (see Prov. 16:28; 17:9; 18:8; 26:20,22).[22]

As you develop your prayer ministry, it is essential to be
aware of the following obstacles to mobilizing corporate prayer
in the church, in order to overcome them:

1. The Church has been inundated with Christian
   humanism (i.e., doing things for God in our own abilities).
2. Prayer is often human centered, not God centered. We
   tend to use prayer as a means to get what we want to
   further our own kingdoms—What will *I* get out of it?
3. Consistent, continual corporate prayer is difficult to
   establish because so much of our praying today is
   dependent on feelings. Prayer-room praying depends
   on a corporate mentality of discipline and commitment. Prayer is a choice, not a feeling. Prayer rooms are
   based on obedience, out of love for Christ.
4. Corporate prayer is work because it has been neglected
   for so many years. There is a huge void in the training
   of ministers in prayer.
5. Prayer rooms are slow to start because people are often
   afraid of group prayer. Fear of failure or discomfort,
   often based on past experiences, can be great hin-
   drances to many people.

6. Prayer for the city in a prayer room is difficult to start because we live in an instant, fast-food society. We want formulas for quick results. Instead of just praying, we want to do something, even if it's wrong. We must not let the desire for quick results cause us to abort a season of prayer that is essential for spiritual awakening in our cities.

7. Prayer is hard to find when there is a lack of vision for church growth. With little vision, there can be little prayer. A vision to reach the city for Christ stretches us beyond ourselves and causes us to seek God.

8. There is resistance to prayer because the enemy hates sustained prayer and will throw every obstacle imaginable in the way of a prayer room.

9. Prayer rooms are hard to establish because churches are often too busy to pray.

10. Collective, consistent prayer is difficult when there is a lack of Christ-centeredness. The main reason we pray is the wonder and revelation of Jesus. You may need to pray for a return of His exaltedness to your church in order to pray rightly. The revelation of Jesus will cause people to want to simply come and sit in His presence. Without such a vision of Jesus Christ, prayer becomes a religious routine, void of intimacy and fulfillment.[23]

One of the Father's most important agendas is for us to spend time seeking Him for the lost and for ways to reach them. When God gives us a great task, He expects us to seek Him with all our heart and soul and strength before we endeavor to do that task. We must realize completely that His Spirit, not might or power, will accomplish this task. One of the fastest ways to kill a prayer ministry is to allow it to become an end in itself.

Once that happens, people will begin to lose interest and the ministry will starve for lack of commitment. The way to keep a prayer ministry going is to attach it to the Great Commission. Prayer is not an end in itself; it is a means to accomplishing the work of God. Remember, our ultimate goal is a harvest of souls, not just well-organized prayer ministries.[24]

Consider this testimony of Terry Teykl:

I remember during one of our first vigils, my time slot was 10:00 in the morning. You must understand that being a fledgling church, our office was a very obscure store front in a small strip of businesses. Yet while I was there praying alone, a young man came to the door wanting to know if someone could talk to him about how to become a Christian. I was astounded. It was our first profession of faith, and it appropriately happened while I was praying, not preaching. I was so moved by the experience that we planned another vigil for the next Saturday, and I signed up again, this time for 4:00 in the afternoon. Again, while I was praying, I heard a knock at the door only to discover another troubled young man who was looking for answers. He, too, accepted Christ, becoming our second profession of faith. For that to have happened once was almost unbelievable, but twice—I knew God was speaking to me. He showed me, "If you will find Me, others will find you." Prayer evangelism works. When we pray targeting the Great Commission, people are drawn to Christ, not by our sign or our building, but by the Holy Spirit.[25]

* The information contained in this chapter was adapted and *used by per-*

mission from Terry Teykl. For further information on this subject of prayer by Terry Teykl, you may write to Prayer Point Press, 2100 N. Carrolton Dr., Muncie, IN, 47304, or call (765) 759-0215 or (888) 656-6067.

Notes

1. Terry Teykl, *Pray the Price* (Muncie, IN: Prayer Point Press, 1997), p. 134.
2. Ibid., pp. 134-138.
3. Terry Teykl, *Blueprint for the House of Prayer* (Muncie, IN: Prayer Point Press, 1997), p. 49. See also Teykl's *Making Room to Pray* (Muncie, IN: Prayer Point Press, 1993), pp. 60-68; and *Pray the Price*, pp. 130-133.
4. Teykl, *Blueprint for the House of Prayer*, pp. 48, 49.
5. Teykl, *Mosquito on an Elephant's Rump* (Muncie, IN: Prayer Point Press, 2000), pp. 47-52.
6. Teykl, *How to Pray After You've Kicked the Dog* (Muncie, IN: Prayer Point Press, 1999), pp. 208-295.
7. Teykl, *Making Room to Pray*, p. 69. See also Teykl's *Pray the Price*, pp. 77, 78.
8. Teykl, *Blueprint for the House of Prayer*, p. 33.
9. Teykl, *Blueprint for the House of Prayer*, p. 33. See also Teykl's *Making Room to Pray*, pp. 77, 78.
10. Teykl, *Pray the Price*, pp. 29-31.
11. Ibid., pp. 31, 32.
12. Teykl, *Making Room to Pray*, pp. 92, 93. See also Teykl's *Pray the Price*, p. 34.
13. Teykl, *Making Room to Pray*, p. 30.
14. Ibid., pp. 75-80.
15. Teykl, *Pray the Price*, pp. 35, 36.
16. Teykl, *Blueprint for the House of Prayer*, p. 31.
17. Ibid., p. 25
18. Teykl, *Pray the Price*, pp. 38-44.
19. Teykl, *Making Room to Pray*, pp. 38-44.
20. Ibid., pp. 80-83, 93.
21. Teykl, *Making Room to Pray*, pp. 86-90. See also Teykl's *Pray the Price*, p. 43.
22. Teykl, *Blueprint for the House of Prayer*, p. 53.
23. Teykl, *Making Room to Pray*, pp. 95-100.
24. Teykl, *Making Room to Pray*, pp. 12, 29. See also Teykl's *Pray the Price*, p. 103.
25. Teykl, *Pray the Price*, p. 47.

Bibliography

Alves, Elizabeth. *Becoming a Prayer Warrior*. Ventura, CA: Renew Books, 1998.

Barna Research Online. "Angels Are In—Devil and Holy Spirit Are Out." April 29, 1997. http://www.barna.org/cgi-bin/ PagePressRelease.asp?PressReleaseID=3 (accessed April 2000).

———. "Annual Survey of America's Faith Shows No Significant Changes in Past Year." March 8, 1999. http://www.barna.org/cgi-bin/PagePressRelease.asp? PressReleaseID=17 (accessed April 2000).

———. "Christianity Showing No Visible Signs of a Nationwide Revival." March 3, 1998. http://www.barna.org/cgi-bin/ PressRelease.asp?PressReleaseID=16 (accessed April 2000).

Beckett, Bob. *Commitment to Conquer*. Grand Rapids, MI: Chosen Books, 1997.

Buckingham, Jamie. *The Nazarene*. Ann Arbor, MI: Servant Publications, 1991.

Bullinger, Ethelbert W. *A Critical Lexicon and Concordance to the English and Greek New Testament*. Grand Rapids, MI: Zondervan Publishing House, 1975.

Goleman, Daniel. "What's Your Emotional IQ?" *Readers Digest*, January 1996.

Hamon, Jane. *Dreams and Visions*. Santa Rosa Beach, FL: Christian International, 1997.

Heidler, Robert. *Experiencing the Spirit.* Ventura, CA: Renew Books, 1998.

Henderson, Solveig and Ken. "Abandoned to Jesus." N.p, n.d.

Jacobs, Cindy. "Healing and Deliverance Through Spiritual Warfare for the Nations." In *Healing the Nations,* comp. John Sanford (Grand Rapids, MI: Chosen Books, 2000).

——. *Possessing the Gates of the Enemy.* Tarrytown, NY: Chosen Books, 1991.

——. *The Voice of God.* Ventura, CA: Regal Books, 1995.

Larson, Craig Brian. *Choice Contemporary Stories and Illustrations for Preachers, Teachers and Writers.* Grand Rapids, MI: Baker Book House, 1998.

——. *Contemporary Illustrations for Preachers, Teachers and Writers.* Grand Rapids, MI: Baker Book House, 1996.

——. *Illustrations for Preaching and Teaching.* Grand Rapids, MI: Baker Book House, 1993.

Lindsay, Gordon. *Acts in Action.* Dallas TX: Christ For The Nations, 1975.

Lindsay, Mrs. Gordon. *My Diary Secrets.* Dallas, TX: Christ For The Nations, 1976.

Otis, Jr., George. *Informed Intercession.* Ventura, CA: Renew Books, 1999.

Remembering Pearl Harbor. Portillo, Michael. "The Attack on Pearl Harbor." April 10, 1997. http://brill.acomp.usf.edu/ ~mportill/assign.html (accessed April 2000).

Rowell, Edward K. *Fresh Illustrations for Preaching and Teaching.* Grand Rapids, MI: Baker Book House, 1997.

Sheets, Dutch. *Intercessory Prayer.* Ventura, CA: Regal Books, 1996.

Sherrer, Quin. *Good Night, Lord.* Ventura, CA: Regal Books, 2000.

———. *How to Pray for Your Children.* Ventura, CA: Regal Books, 1998.

———. *Listen, God Is Speaking to You.* Ann Arbor, MI: Servant Publications, 1999.

Sherrer, Quin and Ruthanne Garlock. *A Woman's Guide to Spirit-Filled Living.* Ann Arbor, MI: Servant Publications, 1996.

———. *A Woman's Guide to Spiritual Warfare.* Ann Arbor, MI: Servant Publications, 1991.

———. *How to Pray for Your Family and Friends.* Ann Arbor, MI: Servant Publications, 1990.

———. *The Spiritual Warrior's Prayer Guide.* Ann Arbor, MI: Servant Publications, 1992.

Stop the Violence, Face the Music. "Teens at Home." 2000. http://www.stv.net/contents/stats/05.html (accessed April 2000).

———. "Teens at School." 2000. http://www.stv.net/contents/stats/04.html (accessed April 2000).

Strong, James. *The New Strong's Exhaustive Concordance of the Bible.* Nashville, TN: Thomas Nelson Publishers, 1990.

Teykl, Terry. *Blueprint for the House of Prayer.* Muncie, IN: Prayer Point Press, 1997.

———. *How to Pray After You've Kicked the Dog.* Muncie, IN: Prayer Point Press, 1999.

———. *Making Room to Pray.* Muncie, IN: Prayer Point Press, 1993.

———. *Mosquito on an Elephant's Rump: A Collection of Articles, Stories and Quotes.* Munice, IN: Prayer Point Press, 2000.

———. *Pray the Price.* Muncie, IN: Prayer Point Press, 1997.

U.S. Department of Health and Human Services. Office of the Assistant Secretary for Planning and Evaluation. "A National Strategy to Prevent Teen Pregnancy, Annual Report 1997-98." June 1998. http://aspe.hhs.gov/hsp/teenp/97-98rpt.htm (accessed April 2000).

Wagner, C. Peter. *Blazing the Way.* Ventura, CA: Regal Books, 1995.

———. "Operation Queen's Palace—A Proposal for a Major International Prayer Journey and Prophetic Act." A paper for Global Harvest Ministries, Colorado Springs, CO, January 1998.

———. *Prayer Shield.* Ventura, CA: Regal Books, 1992.

———. *Praying with Power.* Ventura, CA: Regal Books, 1997.

———. *Warfare Prayer.* Ventura, CA: Regal Books, 1992.
Wentroble, Barbara. *Prophetic Intercession.* Ventura, CA: Renew Books, 1999.

Women's Wire. "Abortion's Unexpected Side Effects?" 1999. http://www.women.com/news/forums/backtalk/E0819 (accessed September 22, 1999).

World Prayer Center. "Celebration Ephesus News Release." Colorado Springs, CO (October 5, 1999).

Youth Culture Department. "Youth Culture Statistics." Focus on the Family, December 13, 1998.

Youthworker. Youth Specialties. "Youth Culture Update." November/December 1998. http://www.gospelcom.net/ys/free/stats (accessed April 2000).

Zodhiates, Spiros. *Hebrew-Greek Key Study Bible—New American Standard.* Rev. ed. Chattanooga, TN: AMG Publishers, 1990.

———. *The Complete Word Study Dictionary.* Iowa Falls, IA: Word Bible Publishers, 1992.

Word Index

Scripture Index

——————————— NEW TESTAMENT ———————————

Best-Sellers from Regal

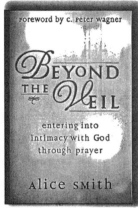

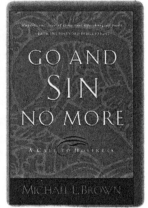
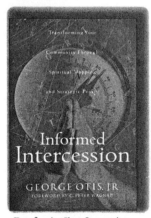
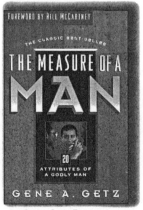
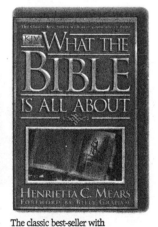

Spirit-Led Strategies for Leading People to Christ

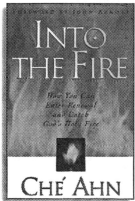

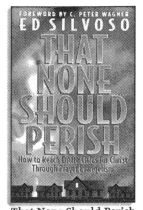
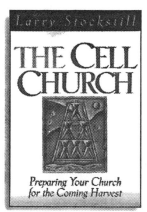